DAVID WELLS'
COMPLETE GUIDE TO DEVELOPING YOUR PSYCHIC SKILLS

DAVID WELLS'
COMPLETE GUIDE TO DEVELOPING YOUR PSYCHIC SKILLS

DAVID WELLS

HAY HOUSE

Australia • Canada • Hong Kong
South Africa • United Kingdom • United States

First published and distributed in the United Kingdom by:
Hay House UK Ltd, 292B Kensal Rd, London W10 5BE. Tel.: (44) 20 8962 1230;
Fax: (44) 20 8962 1239. www.hayhouse.co.uk

Published and distributed in the United States of America by:
Hay House, Inc., PO Box 5100, Carlsbad, CA 92018-5100. Tel.: (1) 760 431 7695
or (800) 654 5126; Fax (1) 760 431 6948 or (800) 650 5115. www.hayhouse.com

Published and distributed in Australia by:
Hay House Australia Ltd, 18/36 Ralph St, Alexandria NSW 2015. Tel.: (61) 2 9669
4299; Fax: (61) 2 9669 4144. www.hayhouse.com.au

Published and distributed in the Republic of South Africa by:
Hay House SA (Pty), Ltd, PO Box 990, Witkoppen 2068. Tel./Fax: (27) 11 706
6612. orders@psdprom.co.za

Distributed in Canada by:
Raincoast, 9050 Shaughnessy St, Vancouver, BC V6P 6E5. Tel.: (1) 604 323 7100;
Fax: (1) 604 323 2600

The author of this book does not dispense medical advice or prescribe the use of
any technique as a form of treatment for physical or medical problems without
the advice of a physician, either directly or indirectly. The intent of the author is
only to offer information of a general nature to help you in your quest for emotional and spiritual wellbeing. In the event you use any of the information in this
book for yourself, which is your constitutional right, the author and the publish-
er assume no responsibility for your actions.

A catalogue record for this book is available from the British Library.

ISBN 1-4019-1167-6
ISBN 978-1-4019-1167-6

Printed and bound in Great Britain by TJ International, Padstow, Cornwall.

This book is dedicated to the memory of my father.
A more spiritual man you couldn't meet. He paid his taxes,
loved his family and lived for the moment.

I miss you.

Contents

Acknowledgments

It's been a journey and one I haven't done alone. There are many people who deserve my thanks: Bill Barrell and David Roberts who fed and sheltered me when I had nothing; my teacher Jenni Shell who saw something and gave it wings; Jenny Greentree for being there throughout the centuries; Star Weavers for sharing the long haul up the tree of life and the joyous flight down; Jane Ennis at *Now* magazine for giving me my break; Karl Beattie, Yvette Fielding and all the crew of *Most Haunted* for the most enjoyable job in the world, apart from Jon Gilbert who frankly only encourages me to eat too much; all at Hay House for being supportive and there at the right place at the right time; and to Moonmonkey, you know what you did and when you did it.

To my Mum and Sister a special mention, without your quiet support I may have done what was expected rather than what I wanted.

My gratitude to you all.

Introduction

Why might you want to develop your psychic skills? There are many reasons. For some people, it's the predictive nature of their gifts that intrigues them; for others, it's the link to their own spirituality. For me, it's a combination of the two. I've found you can take your psychic gifts and mix them with earthly reality to form a plan for your future. That way you can make your life happen rather than simply going along with it.

Tall dark handsome strangers and long journeys are of no interest here – instead it's all about you and your own desire to be all you can be and to create your own heaven on Earth. If that sounds too incredible, prepare to be amazed. Working with these tools in your own unique way will bring about many changes. They may not always be comfortable, but they will be worth it.

Psychic development does take work, unfortunately. If there were a magic formula and all I had to do was utter a few words and sprinkle some herbs and there you were, enlightened and ready to be the best you could be, believe me I would. Of course the truth is that anything worth having takes work, and that's never been truer than of the journey you are about to embark upon.

When I started on my own path I signed up for a six-week astrology course and ended my formal training 13 years later! I'm not suggesting it will take you 13 years to plough through this book - what it is designed to do is give you some insights into what you are capable of, to introduce you to some of the many techniques available and to offer some for you to try so that you can see which resonate with you and which don't.

My favoured arts are astrology, past-life regression and Tarot – and they all work together when you know how. I have added energy and chakra work here, as well as the fascinating art of numerology, to offer you more opportunities to understand your own personal talents and strengths. Then you can use your psychic gifts to build the life you want using the tools you have brought with you to do it. And you *can* do it! Many times I've heard 'I can't meditate' or 'I have no talent in that department,' but neither is an option here! The easy-to-follow techniques in this book aren't about failure, they are about success.

Interwoven throughout the book are some of my own experiences, not just of a psychic nature but about life in general. Is there a distinction? By the end of this journey you too may be making your intuitive gifts and your psychic understanding part of your everyday life.

CHAPTER 1

BEGIN AT THE BEGINNING

When you're a little boy and your grandfather comes to say goodnight to you, do you expect him to come through the wardrobe? My father's father died when I was still a very small child and as I was his first grandchild, I suspect he felt he wanted to see more of me. So he did. Later in my life he would be joined on his visits by a couple of uncles. This was always at my grandmother's house, where I stayed frequently. Nobody else saw them, or at least that's what they said, but does that mean nobody else could have seen them? I think not. What it means is nobody else took the time to slow down enough to see them, to shift from one perception to another.

We are all sentient beings, living, breathing and interacting with each other day in, day out, and as we do so there are odd moments when we seem to know a little more than usual, to have a feeling something otherworldly is going on around us. Occasionally we have proof – always personal proof, but proof nonetheless. Usually we just turn the television up or pop another microwave meal into the machine, get frustrated at the four-minute wait, and then the kids come in, making a mess, and before you know it it's bedtime and oblivion. Is that how you want to carry on? Would you prefer to find out more? Would you like to get to know your psychic self? Maybe you could even suggest a date, say next Monday about 7 p.m., for a chat and a get-together? You have to make a commitment to introducing yourself to your psychic self in order for this to work – without it you are looking for a four-minute fill-up that will leave you wanting more and never feeling nourished.

In a world of ten days to slimmer hips, five seconds to a better life and only one day away from the perfect you, it's all too easy to expect everything tomorrow. One thing you need to know from the start is this: developing your psychic skills will take as long as it takes; you cannot rush it. The real truth is you will never know it all, but what you can have in a relatively short time are increased intuition and the ability to plan your life based on the cosmic signs all around you.

How Does It Work?

'The inner and outer worlds of your reality' sounds far too New Age to start with, but hey, it's the best I can do! If you start to pay attention to what's going on in your head and in your everyday life, you will begin to understand who you are – who you really are. With that under way, you will then notice the hidden signposts that only those who have shifted their perception can see and from then on in it becomes a part of your life, just as it should be.

To help you, have a journal by your side. Make it a beautiful book, one you will enjoy writing in, something that can hold all the secrets of your soul – your thoughts, your feelings and your dreams. This will be your book of life. It will show your own path and, more importantly, when you forget it's there it will find you and remind you of how far you have come and what you have learned along the way.

You need to take the time to write in it, of course. You might be wondering how on earth you're going to do that.

Procrastination is the thief of time; action is the antidote that gives it back.

It seems odd that to get time you have to take action, but think about it and you cannot fail to see that it is a plain and simple truth. Here's a simple technique to get you started:

Write down what you do with your time – as you do it. In a day-to-a-page diary, section off how long you take to get ready for work, the time you spend on coffee breaks, your wind-down time, the time spent in front of the TV and anything else you fill your day with. Do this for one week, no longer – a month is just silly; you will get bored stupid and learn absolutely nothing!

At the end of the week, return to your diary and compile your research. How long during the week did you spend getting ready for work? How many hours were you at work? How long were you sitting comatose in front of the TV? How often did you have 'you' time?

Now be honest with yourself – how many hours did you waste doing nothing in particular but at the same time managing to feel you were oh so busy?

By now you may be realizing that you have more than enough time to keep your journal. But just in case you're still feeling daunted by all the work that may be ahead of you, here's a little exercise that will revitalize you!

📖   What makes you sigh with the sheer beauty of it all? Think beyond the front row of your national rugby team – we are talking art here, music, perhaps simply the beauty of nature. Our world is full of ugliness, full of depressing and full-on mind-numbing, boring, beeping lights that pass for entertainment. What stops you in your tracks? For me, beauty is often found in the animal kingdom – the grace of a horse, the timeless beauty of a big cat, or a small one.

You may now be thinking I have lost my mind, but my point is this: you have probably spent your day on a bus, in an office, in a busy coffee house, wherever, and at some point you have been frustrated by another human being, turned your nose up at an awful smell and come home and watched murder, death and mayhem on television – and that's just the news channel.

What kind of images do you think that has sent to your soul? What has your subconscious stored to play back to you later? What are you thinking about and how is your £100 hairdo after all that?

You can't do it every day (if you can, you're lucky), but find time to walk on the beach, go to an art gallery, fill your ears with music or simply watch a movie that is explosion-free. It doesn't sound like much, but it's one of the best mood adjusters you will ever find.

In the Beginning

After the visits from my grandfather and his sons I began to tell people about them, and lo and behold, they didn't believe me. My grandmother, however, knew I was telling the truth because the messages my grandfather would sometimes give me for her often made her turn her head away from me. I knew then that she was upset and that wasn't what I wanted, so I stopped telling her. But still he came to me.

Slowly my life took on some semblance of normality and by the age of about five or six I was enjoying the schoolwork that now filled my head instead of nightly visits from dead relatives. Things began to calm down and I was like any other little boy, playing and eating, eating and playing!

Then one night I remember someone or something not quite as pleasant as Granddad paying a visit. Something icy was wandering around the room, while under the blankets I was freezing cold and wet with perspiration. I could neither call out nor move, frozen with fear in spite of warmth and familiarity of the fire Granny had lit.

Who or what it was I have never known, but it returned for about four nights and on that fourth night I had a fit – a real-life fit, not a door-slamming, 'the service here is terrible' fit – with uncontrollable shaking and crying, absolute fear and terror, and all in the arms of my granny, who thought I was just being a naughty boy. Eventually, when it was clear I wasn't going to calm down, even after a slap in the face, the doctor was called and I was given something to make me sleep.

That was the last time I saw or felt anything from the spiritual worlds until I was 32.

Between Times

At that time our family lived in a small mining community in the Scottish borders and my father was a miner. When the pits closed, he decided it would be best to move closer to

Dumfries so that he could find work and provide a better standard of living for my mum, my little sister and myself. I am eternally grateful that he did. We saw more of him and our life was made more comfortable through his hard work and selfless attitude.

After a fairly standard education I decided to leave school and join the Royal Navy – hardly the most spiritual of institutions, but it would offer me an escape route and expose me to the world. This need to see more of the planet on which I lived was one of my main drives behind joining the navy – that and just how great I would look in the uniform!

Training as a steward (seagoing waiter), I went to work on several ships and shore bases throughout the UK. One of the highlights was serving on board HMS *Dumbarton Castle* during the Falklands conflict, where I learned that death wasn't always about timing, sometimes it was about duty and responsibility. The next was working on board Her Majesty's Yacht *Britannia* and directly for the Queen in the Royal Apartments. The lesson here was also one of duty. I wouldn't swap jobs with Her Majesty – for one, I couldn't put up with all those hangers-on thinking they were 'all that'. Suffice to say, I asked to leave after just a few months and was happy to be away from it all.

Shortly after leaving the Royal Yacht, I decided to leave the navy altogether and began a new career in hotels and leisure clubs in the food and beverage departments. I went in, did stuff I didn't really want to do, got paid, went home and slept. That about summed it up for years! Until one day it all went wrong.

Saturn Return

In astrological terms there is an event that happens around the age of 28–30. The exact timing depends on your personal chart. This event is sent to help you realize what you want by showing you what isn't working for you. I was around 29 when everything crumbled. At the time I was working in a very swish five-star health club in the middle of London. I was one of two assistant managers and was quite enjoying what I was doing until the catalyst for my next step in life appeared in the form of a new boss who knew little and did as much.

Let's just say it was time to move on, so move on I did – unfortunately to nothing in particular. This is where it really gets messy. London isn't the place to be when you have no money and no job and when you're actually not coping very well. With hindsight it's clear I actually wasn't well at all. Being the brave soldier is stupid when you need help, but stupid was the dress of the day, so I wore it.

My life spiralled downwards. At my lowest I spent a couple of nights on the streets of London with nothing and nobody and no will to get up. From somewhere I managed to find the energy to call a friend who lived in town, and he opened not only his heart but also his home to me. For that I will be eternally grateful. Both he and another kind soul took me in when I needed it most and left me to come out of my depression by allowing me to go into it. Without their roofs over my head and their food in my stomach, I would have disappeared. Angels don't have to have wings.

Slowly I began to get things together. I applied for a grant to go to college and study for an HND in tourism and leisure and was given it. A way out! Once more imposing myself on a friend, this time in Portsmouth and paying rent, I began my rehabilitation into the world of purpose – albeit not quite the right purpose just yet!

Raising the Dead

Studying full time and working 40 hours a week in a kitchen wasn't doing me much good. When I went home to Scotland for Christmas, it all caught up with me and I was taken into hospital with pneumonia.

It was just after Christmas Day when I fell ill and it was New Year's Day before I was fully conscious, so I don't remember too much about it, but I do remember one thing. Lying in my hospital bed feeling very comfortable and for once at peace, I drifted off to sleep but then found myself in the corridor outside my room. While I was wandering around, I was approached by an old lady, nobody I knew, who told me to get back into bed, it wasn't my time. 'Odd,' I thought, and turned to go back as she had said. Then I saw myself lying in my bed, but at the same time I was standing in the corridor!

In the blink of an eye I woke and thought I had just been dreaming. But had this been a near-death experience? The strange thing was that at this point I was on my way to a full recovery. I had been very ill earlier and there had been fears for my life, but not when this happened.

At the time I really didn't think any more of it. I got well enough to go home to convalesce and then after six weeks or so I went back to Portsmouth to try to get back to college at least part time. And that's when it all kicked off.

Things that Go Bump in the Night

Try sleeping when you can hear someone shuffling around your room and can feel the bedclothes being tugged, especially when you know you're in the house on your own. That experience will stay with me for the rest of my life.

Many odd things happened to me over a period of about a month. There was the shuffling, lights would zoom around the room, I would wake up and see faces looking at me and worst of all once I actually felt someone get into bed with me.

That was the point when I thought my sanity was going. I left the house I was living in, thinking it was haunted, and went to stay with a friend, but the faces and other phenomena followed me there.

Shattered, as I hadn't slept properly for weeks, when a mate asked me how I was, I let it all out, crying in my exhaustion. I was really concerned over my own state of mind.

But I was fortunate. Far from thinking I was a Scotch egg short of a picnic, my friend understood what I was going through. A friend of his had experienced similar things and so he knew where to turn. He suggested I called a woman who 'dealt with these sorts of things'. So I did.

Jenni Shell is an extraordinary woman. I had met her many years before at a dinner and thought she was fascinating then. We had exchanged some ideas about life, death and the universe and I had enjoyed the lively debate she provided. With hindsight I realize she had been questioning me about my beliefs even then! Jenni's technique of not saying too much and getting her students to seek the answers rather than just give them is something I myself now use with those under my wing – it teaches rather than just educates. Back then, when her name was given to me as a lifeline, I wasn't that surprised.

'Hello, darling, how can I help?' were her first words. So relieved to hear them, I poured it all out.

Calmly, she told me not to worry, I wasn't going mad, she would help make sense of what was going on – and she did! 'Begin at the beginning' is something she always says when faced with a task that seems daunting, and the beginning for me was sleep. Jenni gave me a visualization to protect me whilst I slept. It was simply to see a five-pointed star burning brightly in my bedroom before I went to sleep, but it worked!

After weeks of no sleep then a straight 12 hours with no interruptions, I simply had to know more, so I called her back.

'Astrology, dear heart, that's what I would suggest. It's earthy and I think you will be good at it.'

As usual, she was right.

CHAPTER 2

ASTROLOGY

The room is full of strange faces and familiar things. There are no pointy hats, no wands, globes or sextants, no telescopes and cauldrons. I'm not sure if I am relieved or disappointed with the ordinariness of it all, but I accept my coloured crayons, ruler and blank sheet of paper and make polite conversation with the new people around me.

The teacher for this evening wanders in, looking more social worker than sorcerer, and very matter of factly tells us that our natal charts are the blueprints of our life and learning to read them will change the way we view the world forever. How true.

It's an odd experience having people who don't know you very well turning to you and delivering a truth that rocks the very inner core of your being, and all from a few squiggles and lines on a circle that apparently have your life mapped out for you, but pretty soon I was returning the favour, albeit a little coyly at first, but what would you expect from someone with Scorpio rising? You see, once you know it, you just can't help coming out with the 'typical Gemini' and the 'That'll be my Neptune conjunct the ascendant' stuff. You watch, you'll be doing the same soon enough. And so a love affair with the mischievous Mercury, the temptations of Venus and the mysteries of Neptune – in fact all the planets and their wonderful personalities, for that's how I see them – began.

The whole astrology thing is interesting to say the least, but where it came from is anyone's guess, as is where it's going. As more and more investigation into the influence of the planets goes on, we learn more about how to use this tool for our own development and to help others.

In an attempt to keep things simple at this point we will be looking only at your Sun (star) sign and the Nodes of the Moon. You will be familiar with Sun signs; the Nodes you probably won't be, but they will give you a lot to think about, that I can guarantee!

Sun Signs

Shall we start with your star sign? We were first split into these 12 sections to make it easier for newspaper astrologers to give predictions based on something that everyone could understand. The Sun moves approximately one degree per day, making it easy to follow; it never moves retrograde (backwards), and everyone knows their Sun sign.

A note to those who find themselves between signs, something I am asked about a lot: my advice is to consider yourself the second sign but also check out the sign above. So if you are born between Cancer and Leo, for example, consider yourself a Leo but keep an eye on Cancer in case it's a particularly good day for them!

Remember always that Sun signs are only a very small part of who you are. There are 10 planets (8 really, as the Sun and Moon are luminaries), 12 signs and 12 sections in your chart, and they all play their part. It takes at least 25,000 years for a personal chart to be repeated perfectly, so you are unique. Unfortunately I cannot write for each individual chart at the moment, so Sun signs and Nodes will have to do until I can!

Aries ♈

21 March–20 April

You are the first born, the start of the wheel, and therefore the sign most likely to be like a baby, demanding attention and constant feeding. That's true to a certain extent! But here we are interested in what makes you tick as far as your spirituality is concerned and not necessarily the way you would approach relationships, career etc. If there is going to be trouble with your psychic development it's going to come from rushing into things rather than stopping and looking where you are going. Hurrying isn't a good idea when you are dealing with the subtle energies of your psychic self, so slow down, you don't want to miss anything!

I know patience isn't an easy thing for you and you are probably going to be frustrated when things won't go at the pace you want. That's why you should consciously take a step back when you find those frustrations moving in on you. Just try it and see!

Meditation isn't likely to be easy for you, as you would rather be up and doing than sitting thinking, which is why you may do better with contemplation. What's the difference? When you meditate, you sit down, close your eyes, tune in and follow what comes up. When you contemplate, you simply think as you do mundane tasks such as the ironing, the washing up and so on, things that you can do on automatic. This does not include operating heavy machinery and driving, as they say with sleep-inducing medicines! What it does mean is you can lose yourself in thought and those thoughts can have as much impact on your psychic growth as visualizing a host of archangels illuminating your path ahead. I have had some very interesting thoughts whilst suffering on the cross-trainer at the gym!

You don't get away with not doing meditation, by the way, just maybe don't do it as often as other signs, as it will turn you off rather than switch you on.

You are likely to be both very creative and very argumentative (both positive traits if used properly), so let's take a look at creativity. It's not always about drawing pictures or making clay pots, it's wherever and whatever you want. That's what creativity means, creating something from nothing, making things happen! To start with, for example, a pencil drawing of your spirit guide may come before you hear or truly see them. If you don't give in to the desire to draw the face, you will delay your growth. Now there's a word an Aries does not like: *delay*.

Astrologically, you are ruled by Mars, and he is impulsive as well as fiery, so why not give in to those creative urges, act on that impulse and see where it takes you? Sit down, light a candle to clear your mind and think about all the positive things your sign brings you and how you can use them in your psychic development. (A few of your traits are listed below. That will get you started.) Remember you are the one in control. See yourself doing whatever you think would help you to advance. You can get a few ideas by listening to what your soul is trying to tell you. If it's to buy that set of watercolours you always wanted, go and do it. If it's to chuck out clutter and free your mind, get the bin-liners ready.

Aries is meant to be in front – just make sure you stay

there and aren't overtaken by those who may have been slower at the start but are more thorough with their preparation.

Aries character traits
Adventurous, courageous, enthusiastic, confident, creative, selfish, impulsive, foolhardy.

Taurus ♉
21 April -21 May

One of my personal favourites! Your sign is one of beauty, inner and outer. It's one where the word 'voluptuous' comes into its own. You have a richness of spirit and an appreciation of the forces of nature that warm those you come across, and on a psychic level you are more likely to be in tune with Mother Earth and Goddess energy than most. That simply means you have more of an acceptance of a female almighty force than a male and applies whether you yourself are male or female.

Practical expression of your beliefs is important and you are likely to warm to rituals such as burning incense, lighting candles and ringing bells. As a Sun conjunct Venus individual myself, I can resonate with that and understand it perfectly, but always have a reason for such devotional practice, even if it's simply to ask for peace for yourself, your family or the world! Ritual without focus is simply a waste.

You crave the safety and security of routine and this can work in your favour in your development if you set aside specific times to study, to meditate or to attend courses about something you are interested in. You do very well with the Tarot, as the stories contained in the deck stimulate all of your senses, making the cards something you can understand quickly and compassionately. Emotion is the key that unlocks the Tarot's secrets.

A relationship is something that seems to provide you with the stability and security you crave. Some signs can function very well on their own, but not you. Those who have you in their life will find you a loyal and supportive partner, someone they can trust and build strong foundations with. This support is doubly important in your own psychic growth, as having that security around you makes it easier for you to relax and to focus. If you do find yourself single, enlist the help of some like-minded mates, as you simply work better when you feel the protection of others around you.

Short cuts are not for you, something that may exasperate the swifter-moving signs, but don't let that bother you. You really must do things at your own pace. Use your natural charms to buy time. These have been bestowed upon you by Venus, your ruling planet, who has decreed you should be amiable and there to offer a shoulder for those that need it as well as often get your own way!

You are not that great at change, but you may cause ripples in your own pond as you grow from being a little fish into a big one, so as you progress, be ready to confront things you would once have left alone. As you change, those around you will change their attitude to you, and this in turn will beget more change. This is the truth of psychic and spiritual development and you will have to face up to it. There is no need to panic, though. Remember, you are never given more than you can handle at any one time!

Taurus character traits
Trustworthy, reliable, patient, methodical, determined, possessive, inflexible, jealous.

Gemini ♊

22 May -21 June

'Versatility' is a word often used when it comes to you, but when does 'versatile' turn into 'having too much to do to finish what you started'? There's something to be said for discipline and for breaking tasks down into smaller modules, things that aren't natural to you, Gemini, but are necessary to make the most of your huge capacity for logical thought. Boredom is usually at the heart of your wanderings, which means preventing it is important in order for you to continue on your spiritual path. I have found the best way for Geminis to learn is to take on more than one discipline at a time. That seems to fit they way they work, but a word of warning: more than one, less than three!

During meditation this boredom threshold will be your greatest challenge and the only way to deal with it is to be aware you are wandering and gently bring yourself back to where you were.

As a sign that's ruled by the element of Air, you are quick-witted and use your mind rather than your emotions. That doesn't mean to say you don't have emotions, it simply means that even if you feel something to the bottom of your boots you won't do anything about it until you have applied your logic to it. There will be many occasions when this will stand you in good stead, but finding a balance where both thoughts and feelings can play their part would be better. Simply stop, look, listen and *feel* a situation before speaking and you can't go wrong!

You are very keen to put your point of view across, but just how keen are you to listen to another person's ideas? On the surface I am sure you will say you are very happy to listen to other people, but then they start speaking and before you know what's happening you can see their lips moving but hear nothing but the voice in your head going 'Me next, me next, me next!' Try to stop for a moment and listen. You might learn something useful.

During your development one thing you really should avoid is giving in because you didn't do something by the book! There are no hard and fast rules to psychic development. Get that message early and you will save yourself a lot of hassle.

You are happy with change, in fact it's more interesting for you than for any other sign, but sudden change is something else. Any problems you may have with it will be mainly due to the issue of control. You make a better driver than passenger, but at some time during your development you are going to find that luxury taken away from you. It's then that you must listen to your inner voice – you know, the deepest of those chattering voices in your head, the one that usually suggests a tougher route! As a Gemini myself, I can tell you from experience that this is one of the hardest things for you to master, but as you become more and more aware, it does get easier.

A journal has been suggested for everyone, but for you it's a lifeline, something you will come back to again and again, and can I ask you to remember that it's a personal thing? Whilst you may want to tell everyone everything, as you develop what you write will become more and more personal, and those you share your journal with at the fluffy beginning of your journey might not understand why they can't see it later on.

Gemini character traits
Flexible, talkative, youthful, communicative, nosy, nervous, inconsistent – oh and fabulous, because I'm one!

Cancer ✤
22 June–23 July

There's an image of Cancer as a bread-baking, home-building, floury-apron-clad family man or woman whose life revolves around the house and kids. A lot of that is true, but here I'm much more interested in you on your own. You are great at giving love and receiving it can be just fine, but what about self-love? Taking time for yourself is crucial to your spiritual and psychic growth and is something you must be prepared to commit to. That means not only taking time to practise and to study but also to simply stop and look around you, to feel the wind and smell the flowers. As tree-hugging as that may sound, it is very important for your advancement.

You have a strong imagination and can see and feel what's going on in full colour, but that very same gift can cause you to worry about things that are yet to happen as well as dwell on things better off left in the past. So stop fretting and allow your intuition to rise to the surface. Over time you will be able to recognize and trust it. The rest is only your conscious mind arguing with your all-knowing subconscious. As you trust your intuition more and more, it will get quieter and quieter. And as you learn more techniques, you will have external proof that you were right to listen to your intuition, and that will help tremendously!

When confronted, you very quickly behave like the crab that represents your sign: you either shut down and retreat into your shell or scuttle sideways to avoid whatever you don't like the look of! Well, 'I'm a Cancer, it's what we do' won't wash here! This tendency is one of the challenges you have to overcome. That doesn't give you a green light to come charging out, claws snapping, either. Just be aware of it as you go through some of the exercises in the book, and be especially aware of it if you are using this book as part of a regular meeting with a group.

Being the eternal Mother, even if you are male, isn't easy and you tend to take on others' problems as your own. This is admirable when you are in a position to help, but ask yourself if you truly are before proceeding. Chances are, you have enough of your own worries to deal with already. Seeing the difference between being supportive and doing everything for someone is usually a good place to start. Just try to be as honest about it as you can.

Change isn't something you care for as a rule, but when you see others getting the results that you would like, you want to follow their path. You're not a trail-blazer, but so what? You don't have to be.

It's normally the commotion involved in change that concerns you, so be gentle on yourself as things move forward. Try to remember that everything will unfold at the right pace for you and those who may be hurrying you along will simply have to wait. In such situations, humour is something you can use to defuse the tension, especially humour about your own misgivings. That's the first step towards self-love – taking the Mickey out of yourself!

Cancer character traits
Emotional, supportive, intuitive, imaginative, sympathetic, moody, sometimes unable to let go.

Leo 🦁

24 July–23 August

'Creative' is the first word that springs to mind with you. The second is 'flamboyant'! You need control in your life and being organized is important. You might not feel that organized, which is exactly why you need it! In order to run your kingdom, for that's what it is, you must know whom you can trust and whom you must keep close because you don't trust them! Luckily that's easy for you, as wearing the right mask at the right time is second nature. As the actor of the zodiac, you have put in many a fine performance!

To be honest, you just love to take centre stage, and drama will always surround you. This can often be a problem for those who know you, but it never seems to be such a worry for you – something I really admire in my many Leo friends. You are able to see through the comedy and tragedy of life and play along or bypass it all and get to the core issue, depending on how you are feeling. Life is for grabbing and you know just where and how!

With your psychic and spiritual development under way you will find a lot out about yourself and having a such strong presence means there will be queues of people waiting to tell you just where they think you are going wrong! Whilst your natural tendency will be to laugh your way through most of it, take some of it home and chew on what you have heard for a while. People say stupid things sometimes and learning to ignore the nonsense isn't something you need any help with. Where you could use some assistance is with learning just what to do with those things that push real buttons in you. As your psychic centre awakens, those buttons will be your signal to look more closely at something.

Change is something you don't really like, but if it has to happen and you can see the long-term gains, you embrace it with the caution of a cat and the courage of a lion. Seeing the challenges ahead gets you excited and gives you something to fill your already busy days with. Doing nothing is a foreign concept to you. I often wonder if that's because you feel that if you stop you will never start again. Rushing around doing this that and the other can make you hard to pin down and this can cause problems when you do any spiritual work in a group situation, so try to remember that even you need to stop now and again.

You are a sensitive sign – you pretend you're not, but we all know you are – and giving in to the emotions you feel rather than trying to brave them out will do you good. As you develop, you will find you want to show more of them. Let it be a natural process. Adapting to it slowly will help you to deal with the inevitable personal changes that an understanding of the psychic and spiritual realms will bring.

Leo character traits
Generous, flamboyant, charismatic, faithful, loving, pompous, bossy, intolerant.

Virgo ♍
24 August–23 September
'Practical' isn't the most glamorous of descriptions, but it fits, and that will reassure you, Virgo. I have to tell you that for the purposes of this book you are likely to be one of those people who will follow things up properly, analyse when it's applicable and worry when it isn't! During your psychic development, a little creativity and a lot of relying on intu-

ition rather than facts and figures will work well for you. If you are working in a group, try to team up with Fire signs such as Aries, Leo and Sagittarius. They will help you and you them.

You are always good at concentrating on tiny details, but sometimes you need to be able to see the bigger picture. This means consciously stepping back, something that's best done by giving yourself a sacred day – a day to lie in a bath, walk in the woods or do whatever you want. It's your day. Make it once a week or once a month – once a year is just plain silly! On this day, think about your bigger plans and look at the fresh understandings that getting in touch with your inner self is bringing you.

You are a hard worker and that can often mean lack of play in your life. Even when it's on offer you may be the first to come up with an excuse for opting out – a mistake! Through lighter times you release the concerns building up and a change in perspective is often the result, so next time you are asked out on the spur of the moment say 'yes'. Not only will you have a good time, but you will be well on your way to slaying a few silly fears about other people's percep- tions of you.

Change is something you understand must happen, but does it have to happen so quickly? 'No' is the short answer to that one. Remember you are in control of the pace and as long as you continue to move forward and not backwards, you can go at whatever speed you want. Setting realistic goals works extremely well for you, as you are more committed than most, especially when you write something down. Where would a Virgo be without a list?!

You have a penchant for pleasing others – in fact that seems to be your greatest motivation. But don't confuse approval with permission. You don't need anyone's permission to improve your life any way you see fit.

Spiritually, you are a sign of devotion, of discipleship, and one that will be rewarded according to the simple equation of effort in, results out. You recognize that very quickly and within group situations you might be a hard taskmaster for those who lag behind. This won't make you very popular, even if you are right! Remember to include those Fire signs in your development. They will remind you that there ought to be some fun along the way, and I would agree with that!

Virgo character traits

Modest, practical, diligent, analytical, intelligent, fussy, scrupulous, over-critical, fault-finding.

Libra ♎

24 September–23 October

You don't like to take sides in an argument, preferring to sit in the middle somewhere, but unfortunately life isn't that simple and fence-sitting is often seen as a way out rather than the honourable activity you are trying to make it. This can often lead to the very thing you are trying to avoid: confrontation.

Learning how to have an opinion and come to a decision is something you will have to deal with early on in your development. There is room for debate – lots of room – but there is a limit to how long people will spend going over the why and wherefore of the same situation and you must know what it is.

As an astrological sign, you are sometimes accused of laziness, and even I sometimes liken Libra to Dylan from *The*

Magic Roundabout. He was the rabbit who slept under a tree for most of the time! Laziness isn't the real deal – you actually have as much energy as any other sign. I think what people pick up on is the 'let it be' attitude you sometimes exhibit, because frankly that's how you feel and what's important to them isn't that big a deal to you! Be aware that others may return the favour if you don't get involved.

A single Libra is like a single swan: there's a kind of melancholy yet serene quality about them, a longing for their other half. If you are single, though, don't worry – you can do just fine! Great friendships are the key to helping you blossom and as a social sign you shouldn't find yourself too short of those. Love does make you brighter, but it has to be said it can also make you absent from anyone's life other than your partner's, and that can be annoying to those who are used to seeing more of you. As ever, balance is important!

In your spiritual and psychic development there is one relationship that is crucial: the one with yourself! The sort of inner debate this entails will produce more questions than you have answers for. It will start with excitement, but that can often dwindle as time goes on. It's here you will need those friends again. They will remind you of just how great you are, and frankly you ought to listen!

As you progress, your viewpoint will change and you will find you take decisions more quickly, simply because you are more sure of yourself and have no need to think things through quite as thoroughly. You have found a balance between your intuition and your intellect and learned to trust it.

One thing that really helps you do well is beautiful surroundings, so make sure that wherever you do your meditation or visualization fills your heart with an appreciation of the gifts of your ruler Venus. A single fresh flower, a beautiful aroma and meltingly harmonious music will all help put you in a good frame of mind and that will in turn will improve your experience.

Libra character traits
Diplomatic, sociable, charming, romantic, idealistic, changeable, easily influenced, flirtatious.

Scorpio ♏
24 October–22 November

The very mention of your sign can make some people pull a face and tell you just how much they dislike it – never a great way to start a conversation, I find! The truth is they don't know it very well. It is a sensitive and tender sign, one that needs careful handling but, if shown the respect it deserves, one that will prove loyal and dependable.

Secretly, I think you enjoy the sort of reaction you get when you declare your sign – 'secretly' being a great Scorpio word! You don't like anyone getting to know you before you have the measure of them and you will guard your right to privacy above all else. It's a rare Scorpio who has only one lock on their front door – two is a minimum, three is the norm! I'm a Scorpio rising and I have four!

Jealousy is perhaps the greatest downside of your sign. Whether it's of a lover, an ex or someone who's doing better than you are, it's something you will be urged to confront as your development goes along, I have yet to meet a Scorpio who has got through psychic and spiritual development without facing up to this one and to the intensity of their own emotions. That said, it's the very fact that you have such sensitivity that makes you one of the most psychic signs in the zodiac.

'Energy' is one of those words that's overused in today's world. You will often hear people say things like 'I just didn't like the energy of the place' or 'His energy was all wrong for me,' but what are they actually saying? You will know what you mean when you say you don't like an energy, Scorpio. You will know it makes you fearful, tense, unhappy, stupid and/or in love! But will you know what to do about it? You will soon.

As you start to develop, your skills will improve rapidly, and no matter what discipline you decide is your forte, it's the one that you avoid that will turn out to be the real star! For me, it was clear from the beginning that I was drawn to astrology, and I love it, but my real psychic gifts come into play when I pick up my Tarot cards – something I avoided for a long, long time.

Timing is everything in psychic development and you will find more than most that you cannot force anything and things will have a habit of unfolding if and when they are ready. Happily, you can accept that.

Change isn't something you like unless you have stability in other parts of your life, namely your home. Without a strong base it's very difficult for you to relax into any inner changes that may be happening to you. So sort out this part of your life sooner rather than later if you feel it's not quite there yet, although for most of you it's done before your mind turns towards your psychic development.

In a group situation, getting things out of you could be like pulling teeth. Try to learn to open wide early on – it will benefit you and those you study with.

Scorpio character traits

Determined, powerful, magnetic, intuitive, jealous, compulsive, secretive, obstinate.

Sagittarius ♐

23 November–21 December

Challenges are what you live for! Firing your arrows into the distance, seeing where they land then simply following them would be heaven! That adventurous part of your nature, coupled with your search for knowledge, will stand you in good stead as your psychic journey unfolds. Books and everything associated with learning melt your butter, and putting what you learn into practice is the toast that you can drip it over!

Setting new targets and figuring out how you are going to meet them is something you share with the other Fire signs, Aries and Leo. The difference between you and them is the seriousness with which you apply yourself, even when the going gets tough. This tenacity, together with that optimistic nature of yours, will help you succeed where others may fail, but this very blessing can cause problems when the practicalities of life get in the way. You can sometimes become so obsessed with a goal that everything else falls by the wayside. Try to maintain a realistic viewpoint with targets. When you are setting them, please put in smaller objectives to get you excited as you move along. Without them, you will only see the destination and miss out on the all-important journey, and that's really the important part in any psychic or spiritual work.

In group work, you will be enthusiastic enough to enrol those who may not want to be enrolled, but they are likely to be caught up in your excitement rather than their own, so please don't be disappointed if they later fall by the wayside. This is something that can upset you, Sagittarius, and you may feel that you have failed because you couldn't encourage them. Before you start doubting yourself, just remember we don't all think the same – thank heavens! Having said that, it works well if you have someone to travel with you on your path to psychic development. They will check your tendency to run on ahead and you will give them motivation when they flag!

You manage change well, but have to have the freedom to express yourself the way you want to rather than adhere to anything anyone tells you. That is understandable, which is why I'm going to ask you to see any words, exercises or suggestions in this book as simply that – suggestions. Nothing is required of you. Everything, however, is useful!

Sagittarius character traits
Optimistic, good-humoured, honest, to the point, reckless, tactless, restless, over-enthusiastic.

Capricorn ♑
22 December–20 January

Well, Capricorn, are you finding that doing the right thing, or at least being seen to do the right thing, isn't as easy as actually getting on with what you want to do? You are often driven by what you think others would approve of or what is expected of you, and to be frank none of that has any bearing on what it is you want – or at least, it shouldn't. Happily, you are likely to be a straightforward and well-put-together individual and somewhere along the line you will realize you are caught up in the illusion of success over happiness and that enough is enough. By picking this book up, you *have* recognized it! Well done, you!

Not always top of the list when it comes to believing in this sort of work, let alone doing any of it yourself, you are someone who will question things more than most – a healthy thing, if you ask me. Please do ask, there is nothing wrong in asking, I spent most of my development asking, and believe me, I kept on doing it until I laughed at myself for it! For you, though, all those questions will really only be answered by personal proof – and no other should matter.

Your sense of humour is legendary. Now, you may think that has little to do with your psychic or spiritual development, but I can tell you that it has more to do with it than you think. The more you work at it, the more you will see that odd, even funny coincidences have more to tell you than those heavy straightforward lessons you are probably expecting. The spiritual realms have a great sense of humour and as a rule the higher the beings you encounter, the more humour they tend to have!

So what's so funny? Could it be the odd mix of confidence and self-doubt you show, or perhaps it's your insistence on the truth then holding back on how you feel about someone or something? Emotions are truth as well – let's see some!

The animal that represents you is of course the goat, but have you ever stopped to consider what that means for you? Sure-footed and able to get to the top of even the most difficult terrain, it tells those around you that you are a capable individual who will succeed in everything you do.

Change isn't a worry to you and as long as you get those proofs you are looking for, it will only beget more change. That's fine – you are highly organized and able to make sure you get the most from any situation. But with this type of development you must know what it is you are aiming for. You will be given the chance to touch what you seek (for that's the only way you will believe in it). Just make sure you aren't too busy planning your next move to notice!

Capricorn character traits
Practical, inspirational, patient, ambitious, cautious, reserved, rigid, inflexible, pessimistic.

Aquarius ♒
21 January–19 February

Anyone who knows you will know you are the independent sort and as such you are sometimes best left alone until you go looking for help. For you, that's much better than being bombarded with lots of offers! It can sometimes mean you are in trouble before you get round to asking, though, which is a little unnecessary and something you are likely to be challenged on as your development progresses. The odd thing is that you *are* a team player. Can this mean that you are more interested in helping others than helping yourself? Think about that one!

You are an original, there will be absolutely nobody like you, and whilst you could argue that's the same for all of us, you know what I'm talking about here – you are unique and there will be something odd about you that makes you hard to forget! This is something that works in your favour as you grow psychically and spiritually by bringing you to the attention of those who will help you on your journey – even without asking!

You can be as stubborn as a Taurus, more so in fact, which will make it tough to move on sometimes in your development. Those who come up against this streak in you should learn to leave you to it until you have come to a conclusion on your own. But please don't dwell in la-la land too long – everyone will get bored!

Emotionally, you may not share as much as some and you prefer to use logic rather than attach yourself too much to your emotions. That will most likely change when you realize that emotions are the key to true psychic work. I bet you're looking forward to that!

Unpredictability is one of your most endearing qualities, but bad time-keeping is one of your worst. Make sure you know when one cuts across the other, especially if you have made a commitment to others that they have honoured and you have not. You won't get away with it more than once. If you are working in a group situation you shouldn't expect everyone to wait for you. What you miss, you miss.

As for change, you embrace it when you are fully informed. When you feel something isn't right and you don't know what, you hate the idea, which is why you must be fully connected to your development at all times. Recognizing why something has changed is usually more important than the change itself, and you are analytical enough to find out. As your intuition grows, the combination will be unbeatable!

You are also the sign that rules magik. No, not a misprint, I am talking about the alchemist in us all, the part that knows how to take lead and turn it into gold, the part that recognizes what needs to happen to make something ordinary in us into something that shines.

There are many paths to psychic development and the best is the one you forge yourself. That's where you really do come into your own. You can clear your own way, but do it with good solid information, good solid training and good people by your side. And then fly and do it your way!

Aquarius character traits
Friendly, honest, loyal, unique, independent, cantankerous, unpredictable, unusual.

Pisces ♓
20 February–20 March

As a child, Pisces, you are the sign most likely to have had imaginary friends and played with fairy folk at the bottom the garden. Whether or not they were actually there, I couldn't possibly say!

A natural intuitive, you are likely to be highly perceptive already, but structure is required if you are to make the most of yourself, and that isn't always welcome, is it? The fish swimming in opposite directions that symbolize your sign are sometimes said to refer to your lack of direction. In fact they probably have more to do with your tendency to solve the problems of others before looking at your own needs, which in turn does mean you have less time for what you want to achieve, hence the apparent lack of direction. In solving this, you are likely to be asked to let go of your perceived responsibilities for others. Does your 25-year-old son really need you to do his washing or is he taking you for granted? Thinking about time for you and time for those you consider important in your life isn't an easy one, but it can be done with some organization and prioritizing. I can hear you panicking already! But the beauty of setting aside a particular time to undertake your own psychic development means everyone knows that's what you will be doing and when. Finding out who does not respect that will be an interesting exercise in itself.

Grounding what you learn is important for you. In other words, you need to have practical applications for it, for example helping others through analysing their situations or perhaps practising hands-on healing, which you are likely to be very good at. With most other signs, it's a challenge to leave the mundane humdrum of modern life behind; for you, it's a challenge to embrace it!

As things change, you are likely to project an image into the future that is probably going to worry you more than it's going to encourage you, which is why you must watch what you are thinking. Any negativity will need conscious reprogramming – something you can do through meditation. Then you can start to worry less and smile more as you bring more positive things into your reality and release improbable fears.

Your spiritual and psychic development is likely to progress very quickly in the beginning and then slow down as things get deeper and more intense. Just remember you will be learning more in the slow phases than you think. Often this is the time when changes are happening at a soul level. It's not always easy to explain or to understand, but it simply means you are changing the way you react to things rather than reacting and learning, which is the way that personality growth occurs. See, you're confused already! But confusion is good. It brings forth questions and that's when you start to realize you are on your way!

Pisces character traits
Imaginative, intuitive, selfless, ethereal, sympathetic, escapist, confused, vague, easily led.

◆ ◆ ◆ ◆

And there you have it, your Sun sign explained – and probably those of your partner, friends and anyone else you wanted a sneaky peek at as well! Now it's time to look a little more deeply.

North Nodes

The Nodes of the Moon aren't really planets, they are mathematical points formed by the Moon's orbit around the Earth's path around the Sun. Phew, have you got that? No matter, what you need to know is they will give you new information based on your year and date of birth, information that goes way back – and I mean *way* back, as far as past lives in fact. These are indicated by the position of the South Node and their impact in this life is shown by the North Node. This is the one we will be working with. The Nodes give an interesting view of the strengths and weaknesses in your chart and also show what you are being asked to develop and what you are being asked to leave behind. You can find out where your North Node is from the table at the back of this book *(see pages 207-9)*.

When you have found which sign your Node is in and read all about it, try to reconcile that with your Sun sign. The combination can be very interesting indeed!

Aries

With the North Node in Aries, you are being asked to develop a more independent nature. That doesn't mean doing things on your own all the time, it simply means knowing your own abilities and having faith in them. When you become self-aware to this degree there is little that can faze you and the courage it brings you is immeasurable. It will also help you to become self-sufficient when you need to be as well as be an equal partner when in a relationship.

What you have to be ready to leave behind is an 'eye for an eye' attitude that will only result in everyone being unable to see where they are going. Instead it would be good to develop a heightened sense of what others see when they look at you. That means you can better appreciate where they are coming from.

You are likely to have had past lives in positions where you have relied upon others, but this time you must learn to stand on your own two feet and to let your personality shine through!

Taurus

Loyalty is something you must both cultivate and expect in others. Sometimes that's only done by laying down ground rules and making bottom lines as clear as you can, as well as taking each day at a time. Slowing down may not be easy for you, but that's the challenge, and as soon as you learn that everything needn't be done yesterday, life can take on a richer quality. Leave yourself time to stop and smell the roses along the way.

Another lesson could be forgiveness. By definition that means there will be those who come along to help you learn it! Try to see that it is crucial to both forgive and forget – one without the other is pretty useless. Once this lesson is learned, you will no longer need to be attracted to situations with 'potential for crisis' written all over them! Just make sure you only let go of what you don't want, though, not the whole deal. For example, you may have a relationship where your partner does something that really irritates you. Concentrate on getting rid of the irritation, not the whole relationship! This may need some work. Keep at it and try not to be too judgemental – remember, if you judge others, you are likely to be judged as well.

In past lives you are likely to have been the supporting player. Now you want equal billing.

Gemini

We all know what curiosity did for the cat, but that was only because it got careless, not because it was curious! Ask lots of questions of those around you – you are meant to. That will help you make up your mind about what's going on, and with a little tact and diplomacy you ought to be able to do something with that information. Communication needs to be of the one mouth and two ear variety, though – in other words, listen more than you talk. That way you really will learn what's going on rather than fall victim to gossip and hearsay.

You have a desire to be right, and there's nothing wrong with that as long as it doesn't become so strong that others get bored with it. If you are ever accused of being a little too righteous, you might want to take a step back and question your motives in your search for the truth.

In past lives you are likely to have been a follower of an ideal, a great truth-seeker who eschewed personal relationships and neglected individuals for the sake of your faith. Time to redress the balance.

Cancer

Supporting others is high on your list, but beware of doing things to please people as opposed to doing what you want to do. Knowing the difference is crucial. This doesn't mean to say that you shouldn't be a shoulder for others to lean on, just don't lose your sense of self. This will not be easy for you, but having a keen sense of how you feel – truly feel – will help.

Also, try to realize you cannot control everything and indeed everyone. A prime example is your tendency to take charge whilst travelling. You *must* have all the passports and even when a flight is delayed you are likely to accept responsibility for that! Lighten up. There are times when events must take their own course and when people must make their own mistakes.

You also have a tendency to make everything seem far too difficult. If you break things down into bite-size pieces, that'll make them easier.

In past lives you were probably in institutions where your every move was controlled: monastic lives, for example, where you got out of bed, ate and prayed at the sound of a bell. This time round there are no bells, just you and those feelings!

Leo

Lucky you! Your challenge is to have fun in life, to embrace it with enthusiasm and even to take a few risks along the way. Does this mean you can look at it as a bit of a game? Who told you it wasn't?

You realize pretty early on in life that everything is up to you – it's you who makes things change, it's you who chooses to worry or not to worry, it's you who chooses the attitude you approach problems with. Be ready to stand up and have the spotlight shine on you! You will be asked to perform for those who need to learn from you and you will teach by example, showing others what a difference it makes when you have a sunnier disposition.

All this will also mean that you have to confront the gloom makers – those who want to cover you in cloud, to hide your brightness! Challenging them will need tact and diplomacy – or brashness! Guess which one you prefer? Do it all without appearing egotistical if you can, as that really will turn people off in droves.

Past lives will have been as a watcher, someone looking at life almost from the outside. Now you have the chance to get stuck right in. Enjoy!

Virgo

If you were offered a job you would really love to do but the company wasn't fully established and didn't have a track record you could look at, would you take it anyway? Taking risks is something you must learn. Calculated ones are fine, but there must be an element of 'let's see' as well.

Your organizing skills, however, are second to none. You are able to make something work where others have struggled, to bring chaos into order and to show others how to do the same. No wonder you are sought after! Of course all this can come at a price. You are a bit of a worrier and details are never right for you – something you might need to learn to let go of.

On a personal level you can be very sensitive, taking every word someone says to you and analysing it until you have made certain there is a problem there, even if there isn't! Deal with self-doubt by looking at what you have already achieved and telling yourself that if you have come through that, you can come through anything!

You have had many past lives where you have not been in the equation, where it has been 'we' rather than 'I', 'us' rather than 'me'. As a result your self-worth needs to be confirmed this time round. Go confirm it!

Libra

Joining in, being diplomatic and being able to have a debate rather than rushing off doing your own thing is what you need to work on! It needs thought and practice to be able to see others as they see themselves, work out what they truly think of you and then make your approach accordingly. And then you need to be prepared to share what you have learned or earned! You may be thinking that you should have something back for all your effort. But think like that and you're missing the point.

Try to curb impulsiveness, too. You may find that if you rush into things you will tread on people's toes, causing problems when you attempt to dance with them later on! Compromise is how things move forward; nothing is gained by argument and stalemate. This isn't the same as giving in. By seeing that, you could save yourself a lot of time and effort.

In former lives you are likely to have been very warrior-like, extremely self-sufficient and a real survivor – all great things, but this time round you are asked to balance that by including others in your life and finding what the middle ground is all about.

Scorpio

'Works well without supervision' is what we want to see on your end-of-term report! Cultivating discipline is important for you, but you can do it as long as you can see where you are heading and what the possible threats are – can't you? You can when you get a plan, Stan. Without one, you are likely to drown in chocolate and big squishy sofas. You really need deadlines. Don't wait to be set them – set some yourself! No matter how small they may seem, they will build into something greater if you persist with them and ask for help when necessary!

As well as asking for help, you must also be open to receiving it from others and be ready to show them your emotions. That's probably all they want in return – to know you are happy. And when you are not, of course!

You can be a stubborn creature and whilst that may work in some situations it could be something you want to get rid of. How you go about that is up to you, but the clear answer would be to compromise when the chance is offered rather than throw your dummy out of the pram. Don't always take the tough route – there's probably an easier one if you look hard enough!

You more than likely had a very comfortable past life, one where material possessions were important to you. Whilst there is no reason why you can't have a comfortable life now, that shouldn't be everything to you! Learn to put your trust in other people and to step out of the comfort zone!

Sagittarius

Being able to see your own future is possible with this North

Node placement, or should that be being able to see clearly what you want and how you are going to get there? Listen to yourself, your inner self, that is, and you will be amazed at the wisdom you appear to hold deep within your being. More importantly, learn to trust that wisdom!

Time on your own is important for this, and Mother Nature is even more important. You have to have a sense of the great outdoors, a sense of no boundaries, and what better way than to physically put yourself in that position? The confidence and optimism this brings will cancel out any worries you may have about what other people are thinking. They will be thinking what they are thinking and nothing you do will change that. Don't allow yourself to be lost in gossip and hearsay. The minute you do, the channel to that higher wisdom you hold will go and you will become bogged down in cappuccino and tittle-tattle – hardly life-affirming.

You can also be in something of a hurry. Curb your desire for answers right here, right now. And stop chivvying other people along. Some will need to take a little longer than others. Respect that.

In former lives you were probably in a teaching role of some sort, one where you were able to second-guess others. Now that isn't appropriate any more. It's all about what you are thinking.

Capricorn

You often gain self-respect from the approval of others, but does that have any real value? If you think about it, that sort of outlook is more child-like than adult. You would do better to reassure yourself that you are highly capable and those who doubt it, doubt it – their problem, not yours! You will prove just what you can do by staying goal-orientated and delivering not only on time but early!

A tendency to hang on to the past will also be tested. The sooner you learn to look forwards rather than backwards, the sooner the shackles of the past will no longer be a part of your life.

Moodiness can also be a problem – one that has more to do with being let down by others than anything you have done yourself. Letting others affect your mood isn't something you want to encourage. So get out and about on your own terms. Yes, 'out and about'. Although staying at home is lovely, going out can be rewarding too. When you feel a little house-bound, you know what the answer is!

Former lives have probably all been about looking after others, nurturing their dreams and ambitions and neglecting your own. Now the cookie crumbles in the opposite direction!

Aquarius

Your way forward is to see the whole picture and learn to be more objective. That way you will soon learn that being part of a team works far better than being the star! This doesn't mean you cannot shine, it simply means you are willing to share what you have and that will bring you rewards and create winning situations all round!

Joining in with groups could range from night school to things that are a little more politically active, and as long as you resist the temptation to have things your way rather than the group's way, they ought to work well for you. You could find yourself more involved in humanitarian projects than most and the plight of the underdog is something you will always be championing. Learn to follow your heart instead of doing what is expected of you. Let go of stubbornness in your ideals as well and you could break years of cycles as an outsider.

In past lives you were probably royalty! Now there's something exciting to think about, but as with all royalty, there may have been a tendency to be out of touch with people – something you can now redress, Your Majesty.

Pisces

Of all the North Node signs you are the one that would benefit most from meditation or any practice that slows your mind down, allowing you to connect to something greater, something that brings you clarity and calmness. By focusing on a more spiritual way of life, you will find a trust that can be a guide as well as a comfort and help you welcome change into your life in positive way.

You have to let go of anxiety and the tendency to over-analyse everything to the point of worry, even exaggerated worry – the worst kind! You also have to check the tendency to find fault with others. When we do that, it's often about something that's actually in ourselves. Recognize that you can use your feelings as a mirror that shows you just what's happening in your own life.

You will probably want to be perfect, but that's a tough act to pull off. The important thing is to simply be the best you can be and to be happy with that. Learn to commit to your own happiness too. When you feel uncomfortable in a situation, have the courage to leave.

In past lives you were probably a healer of some sort, conventional or complementary, in a situation where mistakes were life-threatening. That 'do it right or it may have terrible consequences' attitude may colour this life too. Just do your best and be happy doing it.

Consolidation

Astrology is simple: it puts what you already know in front of you, and when that's done you can no longer escape – you have to admit the truth!

Now you have done that, use what you have learned to your advantage. If you recognize your strengths and weaknesses, you will have a clearer path ahead of you.

- In your journal analyse yourself honestly:

    My weaknesses lie in this area (from your Sun sign)…

    My strengths lie here (from your Sun sign)…

    Lessons to hang onto (from your North Node)…

    Lessons to let go of (from your North Node)…

- Write a passage that describes your newfound information. Read it out to the group if you are doing this with other people to see if they can provide you with any more insights. Headline it: *'This is me.'* For example:

    I have a Gemini Sun and my North Node lies in Virgo. So my weakness is the attention span of a ten-year-old and my head is already onto the next thing before I have finished what I am supposed to be concentrating on right now, but that can be a strength if I make sure my life is full of diversity and the opportunity to get bored is kept to a minimum. I

want to hang on to the attention to detail I get from
my North Node, but I would really like to let go of
the worry I have in getting there! Clearly, my head is
ruler of the kingdom, so that alerts me to the imbal-
ance my heart might be feeling. This all means I am
likely to be challenged where I am weakest –
through my emotions – and boy, has that been true!

Now write a piece about who you are – really, really are. Make it as long or as short as you want, but let it flow. Don't challenge anything until after you have written it. Once you have finished, read it, but don't change it. Put it away until you feel you want to revisit it. If you are working with others, give each other feedback on your essays. Be objective and expect the same in return.

Now tell yourself how positive you feel having done all this work and treat yourself to a bubble bath and something gorgeous to eat. Celebrate your first step towards knowing yourself better and opening up to your psychic self.

CHAPTER 3

MOVING ON UP

A strology put me on the back of my white horse and handed me some belief that would shield me and give me a sword to fight my way through my doubts and the challenges that lay ahead.

The first came from a telephone call from Jenni.

'How is the astrology going, darling?'

'Fine,' I assured her.

'How would you feel about joining my Qabala group?'

'Your what?'

The Word

Forget red strings and over-priced water, stay away from the words 'cult' and 'religion' – even 'faith' doesn't do it for me when trying to describe the Qabala. When asked, I simply say it's a way of understanding the universe and your own place in it. It's not a religion, it's not even a faith, it's a way of looking at the world you live in from a mystical perspective without losing yourself in the floaty wistfulness of some New Age practices. It's about living life here on Earth. For me it's the foundation of everything I believe in.

The Qabala does use ancient teachings, but I'm not going into where it comes from; I'm interested in where it's going.

neant to transform everyone it touches.
ings to our modern world isn't always
.ʋ, but once the techniques are learned (and
..cluded in this book), you will never look at the
.ʋ the same way again. There are some contacts for those interested at the back of this book, including a link to Jenni's own website, where you can find more information on the Qabala amongst many other things.

That first time, off I trotted to a magical house with a knight in red armour in the hallway, rooms full of energy and walls steeped in knowledge and wisdom. This was the home of Maat, an organization that was to be my lifesaver.

What I loved about my time there was hardly ever being told anything. Most of what I learned came through experiencing life and being supported by the information imparted at class every Wednesday for 12 years.

First I began to understand energy, that much-used word! I learned how it made me feel and how I could use it to open up my ethereal spiritual body. You'll find out more about this later.

I was also part of a group of people, which at first I found challenging, as I didn't really do lots of people and having my innermost emotions poked and prodded on a weekly basis was quite uncomfortable! Something I say a lot to those who ask me what they ought to do when they aren't at ease in their learning environment is this: if you don't like it, move somewhere else. A third of the way through my own training I did just that. This was no reflection on any of the talented individuals I started off with; it was more about just not feeling as though I fitted in. I was fortunate enough not to have to leave the school I was in and again lucky to be accepted into another group with eight fantastic women who made me feel as if I was never meant to be anywhere else. There is nothing like support from like-minded souls when you're on this journey.

Before you embark, please try to understand that a lot of your psychic development will come about through your feelings. So let yourself go! Taurus, Virgo and Capricorn especially need to stop trying to rationalize everything. Gemini, Libra and Aquarius will have to slow themselves down a bit. Aries, Leo and Sagittarius, you will probably be good at accessing your feelings, but your energy may be very raw. Don't worry if you have a hot flush or two – they will pass as you get used to it! And finally Cancer, Scorpio and Pisces, you have the potential to really allow the emotion to carry you to a greater understanding of who you are, so go for it!

Remember this journey isn't all about what happens externally; a lot goes on inside you as well. Your subconscious mind will be a great asset to you in making these inner changes. It holds a treasure trove of all the things you have ever seen or done and is waiting to be accessed whenever you need to. The easiest way of all is sitting down and going into the recesses of your mind. Simply put, it's good to meditate!

Meditation

Sit cross-legged in front of a Buddha with your eyes shut and be in that centred magical place within... Easy with three kids at your feet, the washing up to do and tonight's dinner inside the dog!

Of all the things people tell me they can't do, the main one is meditate – but they *can*. With a little practice even the busiest of people find time to tap into this amazing technique. And meditation will allow you to access your inner being, the very seat of your psychic self. But how?

Before that, let's ask why.

Why Meditate?

Relaxation

Relaxation is something modern life has told us means a bar of chocolate and the television. Meditation will be helped by neither, so forget that and learn how to plug yourself into something far more powerful. By meditating regularly you will lower your blood pressure, stay calm in situations that would normally have tipped you over the edge and even be able to cope with the food shopping!

Inner peace

The calm you feel when you know things are going to be fine is worth its weight in gold. You cannot get that calm unless you have gone over things in your mind and balanced that with what you feel in your heart. Meditation can help you do this.

Contact with your guides

I know we haven't really spoken much about spiritual guides and doorkeepers yet, but we will. First it's good to know the way to reach them – and that's through meditation. Your own inner voice is included here too – remember, you have as much of a voice as your spirit guide, and you can really benefit from its advice!

Purpose

There is no point in meditation without a purpose. You have to have some sort of focus to it or your subconscious will simply play and send you lots of pretty colours and a few fairy folk to make you smile. All very nice, but will it advance your psychic ability any? No, it won't.

Your purpose doesn't have to be something grand like world peace. That's fine if that's how you feel, of course, but it doesn't have to be anything on that scale. It can be your own peace, it can be finding the answer to a problem you may be having or it may simply be wrapping yourself in a light bubble and feeling great. Whatever it is, though, do have a purpose!

How to Meditate

There are many different ideas about how to meditate and we will explore some of them here. You can pick and choose – 'try before you buy', if you like. Just remember you are in control and the last thing you should be doing is anything that makes you feel uncomfortable. When I first started meditating I was so concerned about getting it right I couldn't relax for fear I had forgotten something. But there are no hard and fast rules and you are in control at all times.

There are two main forms of meditation: active and passive. They both have their own advantages.

Active

Active meditation simply means taking that path to your inner self when you are doing something else, something that means you are walking about, something like, well, walking, for example!

A great way to do this is to get out into nature, to be embraced by the wind, the sun and even the rain (my personal favourite) and to allow your mind to wander. Active meditation is not to be attempted whilst driving a car or operating heavy machinery, by the way, just in case you thought it would make your journey go by quicker!

This type of meditation is best used for times in your life when you feel restless and sitting still is the last thing on your mind. It can be a fantastic way to get your body, mind and spirit all working together to enthuse you with a life force that's much more about doing than thinking about doing! Active meditation is something you will grow into as you go along – of that I am sure!

Passive

Now we get to the realms of sitting still and taking that journey within in the classic way. Would you like to try it now?

First you need to be comfortable. Find a space you can use time and time again, somewhere you can begin to consider your sacred space. It doesn't have to be huge, just large enough for you to sit down and feel secure. You can make it even more special by having a focus. I use a beautiful Buddha that I bought from a junk shop. His face is serene and that little smile he has reminds me not to take myself too seriously. You choose whatever you want, or if you want anything at all!

Meditation is best done on an empty stomach, as too much food inside you can make you sleepy as well as make your stomach gurgle and put you off. So wait a while if you have just had a meal…

Now make sure you are warm – not hot, warm.

That done, you can begin by lighting a candle if you like. Again this is personal choice, as is the use of crystals. Some people like to hold one as they meditate. I do myself. It's a clear quartz and I only use it for my meditations.

Music is another personal choice. I adore it and use it extensively during my meditations, even making up my own CDs to help me. Guided CDs are excellent as well. Just make sure you like the voice of the person on the CD. If it gets right up your nose, you're unlikely to concentrate! Later on we will discuss a method where you can record your own voice for guided meditations – get excited about that one!

Now decide on why you are there and say it out loud, something like 'I wish to find some inner peace and calm to help me throughout today.'

Take a deep breath in, hold it for the count of three and let it go.

Repeat this simple letting-go procedure three times, each time feeling your body relaxing more and more.

Now tense your entire body and relax. Again, do it three times. You may feel a little silly to start with, but notice just how your shoulders become less tense, your neck feels freer and your mind begins to let go already!

Now see yourself surrounded by a beautiful bright light, a light so bright it seems to be tinged with blue and violet. Tell yourself that this light is sent to help you and to attract positive energy towards you.

Now listen to the sounds outside. Is there any traffic, are birds singing in the trees, was that a siren? Be aware of the sounds, acknowledge them and let them go.

Now do the same with the sounds in the room. Can you hear the house creaking, the clock ticking, the cat meowing? Again, let them go.

Now begin to listen to the sounds of your own body – your heart beating, your steady breathing. Listen to the rhythm of life coursing through you.

Now begin to allow pictures to form in your mind. Take note of what you see and as you do let it go. Hang onto nothing.

When you feel completely relaxed, repeat the words 'peace' and 'calm'. Say them slowly and think of what they mean to you. Of course, if you have chosen something else as your purpose, repeat that instead. Maybe it's a question you would like some guidance on.

Now be aware of any messages your inner voice is giving you. Listen to them, acknowledge them and remember them.

When you feel you are beginning to lose them, it's time to bring your consciousness back into the room. Do it slowly. Wiggle your toes and your fingers, stretch out and don't get up too soon! Focus on something in the room and when you are ready, rise, make a cup of tea, contemplate what you have been told and get ready to be human again!

What if nothing happens? So what? You can do it all again tomorrow and I promise you that something will happen soon enough. Don't get despondent. Some people get full Technicolor visions, some get feelings, some get words. It works differently for all of us, but be assured it will work for you in the way it is meant to.

If things consistently don't seem to be happening, you might have set your expectations too high. Try to be realistic. Perhaps start with a five-minute meditation for a week and increase it to ten only when it feels right. Maybe you would do better with a group meditation. Try a few things out and see what works for you.

There are no failures – remember that. 'Failure' is not a word that exists in your development and certainly not in this book!

So now you *can* meditate. What next?

Guided Visualization

This is meditation with words and it is one of the most powerful tools at your disposal. See it as your travel card to the inner and outer worlds of your reality. Exciting stuff, but before that I'm going to ask you to suck lemons!

Imagine there's a fresh lemon in front of you. Its skin is slightly shiny and it smells clean and full of sunshine.

Now imagine picking it up. How does it feel?

Smell it. Look at the texture of its skin.

Now imagine putting it back down again and cutting

it in half. Expose that vibrant centre running with juice.

Pick one of the halves up again. This time, lick it!

Is your mouth watering yet?

You have just done a creative visualization.

The important point to note is there was no lemon there, only the one in your mind, and yet your body had a physical reaction to it – your mouth watered and you no doubt feel more awake now, just as you would if you had licked a piece of real lemon. Now spend some time thinking about the implications of that...

During spiritual guided visualizations you will be taken on journeys which should feel as real as the lemon just has, but at some point you will be left in silence to hear or see what your own mind produces. That's truly magical!

I think it may be time to have a go. Are you ready?

The best way to do the following guided visualization is to record your own voice reading it or to have someone read it to you as you meditate. Alternatively, you can read it through to yourself, remember it and then go through it again in your mind.

📖   Prepare to meditate as before. In this case your purpose is to introduce yourself to a sacred space outside your normal world. Sounds strange? All will become clear!

Imagine you are in a forest, a magical forest. Sense the forest floor under your feet. What does it feel like? See and hear the animals that surround you. Take note of what they are and whether any have more relevance to you than others. What temperature

is it in your forest?
Is it day or night?

Wander along a path. Take a left or a right and see
what unfolds. Let your own subconscious give you the
images it needs you to see at this point. No matter
what or who appears, acknowledge you have seen it
and move on. This is no time for communication –
that comes later.

Love being in the forest, love the feelings it brings to
your physical self, love the safety and security of this
inner world. This place will become the starting-point
for many of your visualizations throughout this book,
so take your time and get to know it. Spend at least
ten minutes there if you can. You can increase the
time as you become more comfortable with the
process. For now, just feel safe, secure and loved within this invigorating place and enjoy being there.

When you are ready, begin to bring your consciousness
back into the room. Wiggle your toes and your fingers
and gently open your eyes and focus on the here and
now.

The very next thing to do is write down in your journal how
you felt, what you saw and what it all means to you. If you
are working with friends, share each other's experiences
and offer each other insights.

Well done! Pat yourself on the back and go and have a
cup of tea and a biscuit. This little ritual at the end of any
psychic work is as important as the work itself. It reminds
you that you are earthly, something that will become
increasingly important as you go on.

The Subconscious Mind

Your subconscious mind, as already mentioned, holds a record of all the things you have ever seen or done. It uses that information in your everyday life – but not always to your advantage.

Teaching an Old Dog New Tricks

Imagine your subconscious is a great big dog. When you think something, it faithfully goes out and brings it back to you, just as a real dog would do with a ball or a stick. So, for example, you think, 'I'm worried about my weight,' and it brings you back weight worries. You think, 'I'm worried about my job,' and lo and behold, back come the job worries. So how do you retrain it? Can you teach an old dog new tricks?

You certainly can! If you simply act as if you have no worries, you don't allow your subconscious to grab any negative thoughts. This may sound difficult, but it's straightforward if you talk to yourself in pictures! Let's embark upon a journey that will show you what I mean.

📖   Imagine you are in your forest. See the trees, smell the grass, hear the birds. Really put yourself there.

Now walk on through the forest until you see a silver door in a hillside.

Look at the door. Is it plain or patterned?

Let it open and walk into the corridor that presents

itself. Don't be afraid – you are safe and secure.

The corridor is lit by torches. They illuminate silver walls and mirrors. Look at your reflection as you pass by. What do you see?

Enter a room at the end of the corridor. Let the room form in its own way. What period in time does it come from? Look at the furniture, feel the temperature, sense it!

Now become aware of a presence in the room. Is it male or female? Maybe it presents itself as an animal. Don't be afraid, for this is a representation of your own subconscious.

Sit down and look at each other for a while. Respect this being, for they are an almighty creature, capable of bringing you all that you desire. But first you have to know more about them.

Sense how best to approach them. Are they funny? Are they serious? Are they withdrawn or maybe scholarly?

That's enough for now. Thank the person for their presence. Know that they are there for you to talk to when you so desire and that they are a part of you.

Leave the room via the corridor.

Come into the forest and let it fade. Bring your attention back to the here and now.

What have you learned? Write down the form that your subconscious took, the way that it spoke to you, if indeed it spoke at all, and remember any name it may have given you.

Now put the kettle on and make a cup of tea. In fact, make me one too! Remember that by doing such a mundane task you are bringing yourself fully back to the world you currently inhabit.

Analyse what the door, the walls, the reflections the rooms, in fact, anything you saw, mean to you. Remember, it's *your* subconscious. If you are working with friends, discuss what you saw. They might pick up on something you have missed.

It is enough to have made contact with your subconscious for now. Later you will find out how to ask it for help in achieving the things that you desire.

Breaking Habits or Cycles You Can Live Without

We nearly all want to change our lives in some way and glossy magazines and television adverts will show us how, promising us a glamorous lifestyle if we drink the latest alcopop or buy a new sofa. In fact, we are bombarded with images every day. Advertising has cottoned on very quickly to the fact that the subconscious thinks in pictures and it uses that to sell us a lot of rubbish that frankly we could do without. But if a picture of a beautiful person can sell a perfume to you, think what an image created by you for you can do...

Visualization can definitely change your life, but before you rush out to start right away, think for a moment about where you are now. You are a product of where you were born, your parents and of course your friends. A multitude of influences, circumstances and events has made you what you are. Some things are so ingrained in your subconscious that they have become part of who you are. How do you identify what needs to be changed? What if you want to break habits or cycles that seem to have gone on forever? How do you tackle them?

Truth is, you don't! The way forward will let itself be known in its own time. Here is one of the greatest truths you will ever have to deal with in your search for your spiritual self: the law of order and timing.

This simply means that everything has a time and a place. You have probably already found this out in your own life. Have you ever forced a situation and sent things into chaos and only later realized that you would have done better to leave well alone? Consider that spot on your nose two days before you go on the date of the century. Every hour on the hour you rush to a mirror and squeeze it, making it worse, and by the time your date arrives you look like Rudolph with a drink problem and Santa Claus is going to be the only man to look at you. If you had left it alone, on the other hand, you could have got by with a cover stick and a great piece of jewellery to attract attention away from the slight blemish. You might even have got a snog behind the bus stand. You get my point!

We all want things now, now, now, but slow down and trust in the law of order and timing and you will get what you need – and that's often so much more rewarding that what you want.

So how do you recognize whether you are in or out of time? When you are constantly fighting for something, does that necessarily mean it isn't the right time for it? And what about being tested? That often feels like wanting something at the wrong time, but could it just be a way of seeing if you wanted it enough?

This can be confusing and I once thought that there was no way to get this one right, but there are techniques that can help you to see more clearly.

📖 Prepare to meditate as before.

Now breathe deeply. Inhale and exhale at a pace that suits you and become aware of your own body.

Focus on your head. Feel the activity that is going on in your brain. Don't analyse anything, just feel the buzz.

Now let your brain get on with it. That hive of activity is not your concern right now.

Now focus on your forehead, right between your eye-brows and in the centre of your forehead.

Imagine you have an eye there – that's right, an eye – and see it in your mind as a closed eye.

Now visualize it opening slowly, just as your own eyes do in the morning.

Allow it to open and, as you do so, consider how useful a third eye would be!

You might see some flash images during this visualization. If you do, try to remember them but don't follow them, just log them in that busy head of yours.

Now close your third eye, return your consciousness back to your brain and get busy again!

Open your real eyes, get that kettle on and help yourself to a chocolate biscuit.

You have just activated, albeit slightly, your third eye chakra. Your what? You'll find out more about that in a moment. For now, experiencing it without the intellectual knowledge is important, just as it was for me.

Now what did you see? What does it mean for you and how can you manage to keep that perception? Write down what you saw or felt and discuss it with your mates if you are doing this with a group.

Do this visualization whenever you feel sluggish and blocked in your 'sight'.

📖   Let's look at a magical way to use a mirror.

Sit in front of a smallish mirror, a shaving size will do. Make yourself comfortable and take a couple of deep breaths.

Don't do this on a bus, by the way – you will be put off at Piccadilly and made to walk the rest of the way!

Now position the mirror so that you can only see yourself from the eyes up.

Ignore the fact that your eyebrows need plucking. In fact, ignore your eyebrows altogether.

Now look into your eyes. Look deeply, beyond the colour and shape. Look beyond your eyes, if you like.

You may be startled at the intensity of this very simple exercise. I will tell you why that happens in a minute. For now, spend no more than five minutes just staring into your eyes.

Now put your mirror down and write down anything you felt or indeed saw in your eyes. Although we are still really dealing with the realms of the personality here, you have just touched on your soul, which is why this can be very intense.

This exercise can also be used to contact your subconscious. Just remember to state your intention as appropriate. And always do it with reverence – you don't want to upset that great big dog!

Getting Off the Treadmill

By now you will have realized what you need to change and hopefully you will be well on the way to figuring out how to go about it, but don't jump the gun. Give yourself time to watch your life. Observation is a great thing when you know what you are looking for and when you have three eyes to do the looking for you!

I am going to ask you to identify just one thing that you do that you would rather not, thank you very much, and to do something that sets things in a different cycle. What that is is up to you. Things like not berating yourself all the time, not moaning at work and not putting off that discussion with Wayne Slob about his lack of libido are all good starting-points!

Once you have decided what to do, how can you prevent negativity from turning your intentions away from fruition? How can you stop those gremlins from telling you how much of a failure you are?

There is no one technique that will guarantee this, and positive thinking isn't always easy after years of the opposite, but it can be done! And now that you have a greater under-standing of the importance of thoughts and words, you will understand how effective it can be.

I am going to show you one technique here, but it's the whole process of detoxifying your spiritual self, of purging yourself of bad habits, negative thoughts and acting out of time with your universe that will make the difference!

Here we go then.

 Get ready to meditate.

See yourself at a cinema. Make it a private fabulous one, not one with nachos stuck to the seat and someone behind you making a model of the Eiffel Tower out of crisp packets.

You are alone in this cinema. Sink into the gorgeous deep comfortable chair and look at the screen.

On the screen see negative thoughts as a shape or colour, or perhaps the words themselves. Just let them take shape in front of you.

Now hear trumpets sound as positive energy comes in to win the day. What is it that comes to your rescue? It can be a person or an animal, a colour or a shape. Just go with what you get and interpret it later!

Remember what you see. Watch it conquer the negativity.

Now let the screen go blank and return your conscious-ness back into the here and now.

Make the tea and eat the biscuits.

Draw your positive symbol in your journal. Colour it in, make it real.

Whenever you have a negative thought – 'I can't,' 'I shouldn't,' 'That's not me,' 'I'm too fat,' 'I'm too old,' whatever it is – see your symbol and let it destroy that thought for you.

Although this is not easy to begin with, the more you use it, the more automatic it becomes. It has been one of the most effective tools that I have found in conquering negative thoughts. When you use it often enough, the symbol seems to appear before the thought in the end!

By now you are probably beginning to understand there's more to psychic development than simply learning the techniques and memorizing the names of planets or when Aries ends and Taurus begins. It's actually about the inner you meeting the external world and the external world's impact on the inner you. So begin to think *outside* what you see and hear. Begin to think about what's actually being said and what you are truly seeing, or in some cases preventing yourself from seeing.

You should also be establishing that all-important contact with your subconscious, the part of you that will help keep you positive and forward-thinking as well as being your psychic personal shopper, able to bring to you all your heart's desires. Some effort will be required, of course, but a lot of it is about meditation and visualization, so get this tool under your belt and you're off and away!

CHAPTER 4

ENERGY

Everything is energy. Have you got that? You, me, this book, the computer, the cat, the hat on the cat, the mat on which the cat in the hat sat – the whole lot. This book is not, however, about physics, it's about psychics, so that's enough detail for now. Just take it as read that everything is energy and energy is a force that can be changed.

This means you can change what happens around you. We're not in the realms of the *Charmed* ones here and there are limits, but essentially you can transform your tiredness, chase away your apathy, calm yourself down or even become more likely to go the gym instead of eating a chocolate bar if you learn how to recognize and use your own personal energy.

You will have felt your own energy already in the meditations you did in the last chapter. That's why I put them first – I wanted you to have some sensations and therefore validate what you felt.

So. Energy. You can feel it. How does it work? How do you use it?

The Chakras

The Sanskrit word *chakra* means 'wheel' and the chakras are literally that, wheels of energy that sit in your aura, or energetic body, the one that surrounds your physical one, the one that goes 'Ouch!' when you hear bad news, tingles when you feel love or just picks up on an odd atmosphere when you are in a haunted house!

There are thousands of chakras on your energetic body, 88,000 to be exact, but just for now we will concentrate on the main seven running from the base of your spine to your crown.

📖 Place your hand over your heart, about four inches over it. What do you feel? Can you feel the flow of energy?

Now move your hand to the right away from your heart. Can you feel the boundaries of your heart chakra? If you can, consciously think about your chakra opening up and then see if you can get it to meet your hand.

Do the same with your crown, your throat, your belly button. What do you feel, where do you feel it the strongest and is there a direction to the energy, is the wheel spinning clockwise or anti-clockwise?

In males, the base chakra tends to rotate clockwise. In females it's anti-clockwise. Then the spinning alternates in each chakra as you come up your body. This is important to note when working with these portals to your energy.

If a chakra isn't working well, it can affect the one above it. Sometimes the best plan is to rebalance them all as often as you can to keep yourself in peak condition. We'll come to that later. For now, it's time to be formally introduced to the seven great wheels that govern your wellbeing!

The First Chakra
The root centre, the base chakra

- Element: Earth

- Colour: Red

- Associations: Physical wellbeing; all solid parts of the body such as bones, teeth and nails, as well as blood and the waste-disposal system. Material security; the drive to succeed.

• Working well: You feel connected to the Earth, to nature, animals and plants. You feel part of the whole, not detached from the rest of life on Earth. Usually you have a good grasp of finances and good physical wellbeing.

• Out of balance: You are possessive and over-indulgent with food, sex and alcohol, as well as obsessive about your security. Everyone may seem to be against you and trust is a foreign concept.

• Balancing: Wear the colour red, especially red knickers! Get out and see the sun set or rise, remind yourself of all the beauty in the world and above all eat good-quality organic food. This chakra must work well for your psychic development. Without good grounding and a positive outlook, your concentration will suffer.

The Second Chakra
The sacral chakra or cross centre

• Element: Water

• Colour: Orange

• Associations: The pelvis, reproductive organs, kidneys; liquids such as gastric juices and lymph; the regulation of the female cycle and the male sperm. The creative process of reproduction.

• Working well: You feel connected to the creative energy within you and express that with confidence to those you love. You are also genuine in your feelings and your actions.

• Out of balance: You are sexually repressed and perhaps have a feeling of unworthiness and a tendency to push away those who could love you. Or maybe the other extreme is prevalent and you use sex as a drug, a way to hide away from the world.

• Balancing: Meditate under a full moon. Let her pull on this chakra and remind you of the ebb and flow of life. Sit by water and listen to its ever-changing rhythm. Wear orange – once more, knickers are good. Just make sure they are Bridget Jones size and come up to your navel!

The Third Chakra

The solar plexus or navel centre

• Element: Fire

• Colour: Yellow/gold

• Associations: The lower back, digestive system (not digestive biscuits!), the stomach, liver and spleen. This chakra is where we shape our wellbeing, taking in goodness to turn it into energy. It's the home of our belly button, the source of life when we are in our mother's womb.

• Working well: You feel at peace and in harmony with yourself, happy with life in general and content with who you are. You also accept others for who they are without judgement. You are happy to accept that good things happen and you are going to have your fair share of them, thank you very much!

• Out of balance: Instead of seeing the glass as half full, you see it as half empty. Your personality is suppressed in some way. You would prefer to be in a dark room with a bar of chocolate and a copy of Woman's Weekly rather than being outside greeting a new day.

• Balancing: Feel sunlight on your face, place yellow flowers around the house, wear a yellow shirt or listen to fiery music. Burn rosemary or bergamot – these oils are infused with the warmth of the sun and its life-giving energy.

The Fourth Chakra

The heart chakra or centre

• Element: Air

• Colour: Pink or green

• Associations: The heart and upper back, including the lower lungs; the circulation of blood and the skin. Devotion and self-sacrifice. Perfect union through love, touch and feelings.

• Working well: You feel divine love, have the ability to change people's understanding and the world around you, and radiate warmth and happiness – clearly something to aim for! You view personal and world events from a platform of love rather than confusion.

• Out of balance: You are always there for others and not yourself. You give love in order to receive something for yourself. You give away your own power and allow someone else to control your destiny. Physically, you may even feel pain in the heart area for no medical rhyme or reason.

• Balancing: Walk in green countryside, carrying a piece of rose quartz or jade or pink roses, and if you have the urge, why not burn some rose oil? It's not the cheapest, but worth every penny.

The Fifth Chakra
The throat chakra, the communication centre

• Element: Ether

• Colour: Pale blue and silver

• Associations: The neck, throat and jaw, ears and voice, upper lungs, arms and thyroid. Communication, self-expression, inspiration. A bridge from the heart to the third eye chakra, linking thoughts and feelings.

• Working well: You express your thoughts and feelings without worrying about being judged and can show your fears and your hopes in equal measure. Your inner honesty is shown by your bearing and your manner.

• Out of balance: Round-shouldered, you hide in the shadow of what you might have been and deny your thoughts or feelings, often using one to suppress the other. You shy away from expressing your dreams to those who could help or share them.

• Balancing: Gaze at a cloudless blue sky, wear silver jewellery, vibrate the vowel sound 'eh' in your throat. Burn sage or eucalyptus. Both may catch in your throat to start with, but that's the point! Wear a blue or silver scarf.

The Sixth Chakra

The third eye chakra, the command chakra

- Colour: Indigo and violet

- Associations: The face, ears, nose, eyes and nervous system; the pituitary gland (the one that tells all the others what to do). The knowledge of your being. Higher knowledge and flashes of inspiration, imagination and intuition – your psychic sight.

- Working well: You have an active mind and advanced knowledge, usually with a spiritual edge, good visualization in meditation and the ability to decipher the symbolic language of the subconscious. You also experience clairvoyance and second sight. Clearly, this is important for your psychic development.

- Out of balance: You over-emphasize thought at the expense of emotion and can seem cold and unapproachable to others. Alternatively, imagination can take over from reality. Some people overdo work on this chakra and end up unable to concentrate on life here on Earth. Balance is the key.

- Balancing: Look at the night sky, see the stars and contemplate what they mean. Astrology can help you bring your divinity to Earth via third-eye understanding of the astrological symbols. Jasmine and mint oils sharpen the senses and open up this chakra. Lapis lazuli can stimulate intuition and bring inner sight.

The Seventh Chakra
The crown chakra or thousand-petalled lotus

- Colour: Violet, white and gold

- Associations: Cerebrum, pineal gland; inner sight, connection with your higher self as well as the universal energies; limitless possibility; radiating energy from the divine through the physical.

- Working well: Your spiritual and earthly life mingle and mix beautifully. There is no end and no beginning to either. Your personal ego is transformed into humanitarian understanding and therefore the full acceptance of all. You can see through the illusions that life brings.

- Out of balance: You feel uncertain and lack purpose. You are lost in the woods. Sometimes ill health happens to stop you in your tracks and force rest and recuperation.

- Balancing: Spend time alone in any beautiful place, preferably as high as you can get without flying. A mountain or hilltop is great if you can find one that's easily accessible! Amethyst and rock crystal stimulate your higher self, helping to connect you to the power of your psychic self. Burn olibanum resin for its uplifting qualities, particularly during meditation.

There are many ways to learn more about these powerful tools – too many, to be honest, which is why I'm just going to share with you a couple of my experiences and a simple but highly effective meditation for sensing what's going on with your own chakras and maintaining them properly.

Constant headaches used to dog me. I couldn't go more

than two days without one. Friends would cite chocolate, coffee, stress and the occasional sweet sherry as the reason, but no matter what I cut out of my diet or lifestyle, they persisted.

I was some way through my own training at this point, that needs to be said, and at class one day my teacher noticed I wasn't my usual chirpy self and asked why. I told her I had a headache, a severe one at that, and she asked how long it had being going on, to which I replied, 'Years!'

Then she asked if I had any odd sensations in my third eye. I had been feeling as if someone was pushing their finger into the middle of my forehead so, excited, I asked if the headaches were a result of my third eye opening, but my teacher replied with a curt and simple 'No!'

How gutted was I? There I was, thinking my third eye was about to be opened sky high, and she said no! Instead, she asked me to remember her teachings earlier that year. Then I remembered that the cause of a problem can sometimes come from the chakra above. So was it my crown chakra that was causing problems? My teacher confirmed that it was.

I went away and thought about my life – my 16-hour working days, my concrete-surrounded living conditions and my rubbish diet – and then I thought about what my crown chakra would ask for if it had a voice.

'I would like some good-quality sleep, some fun in my life and a room for meditation and contemplation. A little bit of recognition for my efforts would be good too. How about taking me out for the day and exposing me to clear blue sky and fresh air?'

So, off I went to a beach near where I was living and walked along it, thinking about how my energy was mixing with the elements and how they fed me and I them. Then it was time to climb up to a higher vantage-point and sit facing into the wind and out to sea. There I opened up to the universe through my much-neglected crown chakra, and kaboom! Great word that, it brings back comic-book stories where sudden explosions leap from the page, which just about describes what happened to me! My head cleared, my vision cleared – why, even my sinuses cleared!

From that day to this I listen to my etheric or energy body and I am aware when something isn't right and do what I can to make it better.

My energy body was also affected when my father died after a long illness and unfortunately I wasn't with him when he crossed – or was I? My sister had called me to say he had gone downhill rapidly and it would be best to get home as soon as I could. Of course I dropped everything and set off on the 400-mile drive back to Scotland. My sister was in touch off and on as I drove up the motorway. At about 4 p.m., out of nowhere I felt as if someone had punched me in the chest. My heart chakra was ripped open and I felt my Dad leave my energy. At that instant I knew he had died. It was hardly a surprise when my sister called a little while later to confirm it.

To those who say the chakras and aura don't exist, I would say you're not listening to the physical world or the spiritual one. They are entwined, whether you like it or not. Why not try this simple meditation and see what happens?

📖 Prepare to meditate as before. Get comfy and remember to set your intention. On this occasion it's to review and balance your chakras.

Breathe in and out three times, On each out-breath release tension. Let the stress and strain of daily life simply fade away.

Relax your body, close your eyes and get ready to move into your magical forest.

As before, see the forest, sense it and be a part of it all.

Let an animal guide come to you. Recognize them and follow them down the path. It begins to move down a slope, gently at first and then quite steeply. Keep up with your guide. They are excited about showing you a special place, a place where you can recuperate and top up your energy by reconnecting with your own etheric body.

Follow your animal until the ground beneath your feet turns from grass and earth to sand and sea. Look up and see a sparkling ocean and a golden beach ahead of you. Allow yourself to paddle in the water, to splash and play. Dance if you feel so inclined.

Now move to the end of the beach where you will see a small hut made of palm fronds and seashells, a place that looks fragile but somehow safe and welcoming. Go inside this simple but very special structure.

There you see a chair. Sit on it and gaze around you. You will see that the walls of the hut are covered in every kind of crystal you can imagine, all mixed up so that they sparkle with every colour of the rainbow.

As you make yourself comfortable on your chair, darkness falls inside the hut. Then a faint red glow begins to emanate from the walls. Let that light fill the space. Allow it to penetrate your body. Watch as it goes in through the first chakra, your base chakra. Watch as it activates the chakra and see how readily the chakra absorbs the energy. Only do this for about a minute or two – you don't want to overdo it!

Now the light turns orange and begins to move to your second chakra, the sacral centre. As it does so, allow it to enter and again let it vibrate through you for a minute or two.

It's the turn of the third chakra now. See the light entering your solar plexus. See it as a bright golden light and let it work its magic. How does it feel?

After a few minutes move on to your fourth chakra, the heart one. Let pink light enter your heart and bathe it for a minute or two. Again remember how you feel if you can.

Now on to the fifth chakra, the throat. Imagine a bright blue light entering to stimulate and correct or enhance this chakra.

As the light turns indigo blue, see it on your sixth chakra, the third eye, and let it gently wake up this centre for second sight.

Finally, allow your attention to move onto your seventh chakra, the crown, and let it be flooded with violet light tinged with gold. In fact, why not let this light go in and out at the same time? See it as a two-way thing connecting you with the universe and the universe with you.

Now watch as the hut fills with all the colours of the rainbow. Bathe in them for a minute or two and as the light dims make your way to the door and back out onto the beach.

How do you feel walking back along the beach? You should be elated, connected, calm, positive, determined, loved, loving and ready for anything!

Follow your animal back to the forest and back to your starting-point. Thank your special little creature and let them and the forest fade as you bring your consciousness back into the room.

Wiggle your toes and fingers, open your eyes and pop the kettle on.

As you sip your tea and eat your biscuit, spend some time writing in your journal. Notice what you felt about each chakra. Which ones felt out of synch? Did any feel overactive, and if they did, what can you do about correcting them?

You should be feeling more balanced and ready for anything now. Just remember how that feels. As you progress that should be the norm rather than the exception.

A word about grounding

Now you have learned how to float off you must think about how you come back to Earth. Remember you need to live here, so it's kind of important!

There are three things that really ground you: eating, drinking and sex! One or all three is great. This is why I recommend a cup of tea and a biscuit – you may have other ideas!

Sometimes I see people who are doing too much work on

their psychic selves with the result that they forget to pay the gas bill, wander around in a daze or just can't sleep for seeming too highly aware. Prevention is better than cure, but if you do overdo things, here's some good advice that was given to me when I did it: eat good organic food and plenty of it, put a teaspoon of salt crystals in your bath, do some gardening, get out into nature and, if you can, have an early night with someone special!

Consolidation

 Draw a little body in your journal or on a piece of paper.

Now colour it in with the relevant chakra colours in the right places.

Now put a plus or a minus on each chakra based on your meditation and what you feel to be right.

Now write down what that tells you about yourself and what you can do about it. Be frank – there's no point in being fluffy about this sort of stuff.

If you are working with a group, make sure you share your drawings with each other and be ready for that all-important feedback. Remember, it's about your chakras, not your artwork!

☆ ☆ ☆ ☆ ☆

CHAPTER 5

PAST LIVES

A friend of mine asked me round for a coffee one morning and, unlikely to turn down the opportunity of a slice of cake, off I went. We were chatting away as you do when she said that another friend of hers would be along in a minute, someone who was also learning the Qabala but was a couple of years ahead of me in her training. 'Nice,' I thought, more interested in my fudge brownie than anything else, to be honest.

Then she arrived. My head spun, my stomach twisted and my reality shifted to another time and place. I was introduced, but could barely talk, and just why was the room filling with what seemed like white mist?

Such was the intensity of this first meeting that the friend who had asked me round for coffee, a very sensitive psychic, left the room as she was becoming affected by the energy.

To this day I swear I knew this new person's name from another life. Even though I knew it was Jenny in today's language, that wasn't what I was hearing. When I told her some time later, she confirmed that name from a former life and told me mine from that self-same life. Later we would both discover something else about our connection and would visit a past life together.

More on that later, but first a look at this fascinating subject.

Past-Life Regression

So there I was, lying on the floor of a charming lady called Anne, looking at her figurine of a dog, or was it a sheep? Not sure. Anyway, it was there in my vision and somewhere in my ear Anne's voice was asking me to imagine simple things like the roof of my house and the garden surrounding it, when wham, I was confronted by the rising mass of an army and there I was with a sword, a shield and not a lot else to defend myself with! More of that later. My point is that in the normality of a suburban house, complete with sweet old lady and china memories, I was not there, I was somewhere else completely, seeing it, smelling it, hearing it and even feeling it. So how come?

People will explain away past-life memories in many ways. Some say they are illusions conjured up by our own subconscious, while others say they are put there by therapists. Of course the obvious explanation is that they are indeed past-life memories. You make up your own mind. Just to clear up one thing, however: it's an urban myth that everyone remembers lives in which they were famous historical personages. I have done many past-life regressions for people and had many of my own, and I can tell you that famous ones are very few and far between. I have never come across a Cleopatra, George Washington or Jesus in all the years I have been doing this. And even when a famous historical life is remembered, the people concerned are usually very humble and not at all given to over-inflated egos.

Enough about fame! Here are some of the other questions that people often ask about past-life regression, together with some answers, of course.

How Do I Know I've Lived Before?

Does another country or a particular era fascinate you? Perhaps your house is already like a step back in time. Maybe you have a special fondness for fashion from another time. Some or all of these could be a link to another life. Alternatively, they could simply mean you read a lot. You decide!

Where Do the Memories Come From?

The memories are stored in your subconscious – the part of you that remembers everything you have ever done. It also has a direct line to your soul, only it's a line that's sometimes blocked by all the nonsense of modern existence. Past-life regression opens the link up again and allows information to flow freely. It's information you will undoubtedly find useful as well as extremely uplifting. Of all the esoteric techniques I use, this one is my one-stop solution, and it can uncover more than just past lives. More on that later.

Can You Get Stuck?

'No' is the short answer to that one. What you may experience after a past-life regression is an adjustment as you come to terms with what you have experienced. For me this meant a deep peace through knowing I had indeed lived before and that whilst things can seem important at the time, really nothing is that important in the great scheme of things. If anything, rather than getting stuck, what you actually do is move on.

One side-effect you may experience is a temporary feeling

of heaviness. This is nothing to worry about and it will leave you very quickly. It's a bit like being rudely awakened when you are in a deep sleep – that heady 'can't co-ordinate brain and limbs' sort of thing.

What If Children Remember Other Lives?

If you have children in your life they may sometimes refer to former lives by saying things like 'My other mummy didn't give me porridge for breakfast' or talking vividly about another place in time when you know they haven't been exposed to that sort of information.

What do you do? That's up to you, but my advice is to ask simple questions that will get more from them, then return to your normal routines. Children will soon lose these memories, which is a shame, but part of me also thinks that's the right thing. That way they learn to live their current lives and their former memories will return to them if they are relevant.

What Are the Akashic Records?

Not a pop band, these are more like a cosmic library. You can use them to review your own personal journey in a much more intellectual rather than emotional way. This is the route I tend to take people on in group regressions, as it brings the mind into play rather than the emotions, making everything much easier to control.

Later you too will take the path that will lead you to these records. The special library where they are housed is a place you can visit as often as you like, as long as you truly give yourself time to think about what you learn there and don't just go for a look-see. I warn you that if you visit without taking it seriously or go too often without doing anything with the information you receive, you will find the door locked and your library card taken off you until you sort it out!

Who Are Soul Mates?

This often misunderstood phrase refers to people who may have travelled with you for a long time, through many lives, interchanging roles so you can both learn whatever it is you need to know to advance your soul.

Do you remember Jenny from earlier? She and I visited Anne for a past-life regression, the difference being we were regressed together to a life we both knew we had shared but wanted more information about. During the regression the extraordinary proof for me was when Jenny would say something that I too was seeing. How could she unless she was indeed remembering a past life we shared?

That life is very personal to both of us and what happened is irrelevant to anyone other than us. The point I want to make is that soul mates don't have to be anything other than friends in this life. A soul mate can be a partner, but that isn't always the case. You will have lots of soul mates – your mum, your auntie, your best friend. Whoever they are, they are someone you love regardless of the sometimes strained relationship you may have and someone who will be the first to help when you are in need.

The what, when, who and why of the people in your life now can be found through past-life regression. If you find no link, this may be a first meeting. Tread carefully and be mindful of the karma you might be creating! Which brings us to...

What Is Karma?

Karma is one of those words that's bandied about willy-nilly. You hear people going on about 'bad karma' and how their deeds will be punished in another life, blah, blah, blah. The truth of karma is simply this: for every action there is an equal and opposite reaction and they all happen without judgement. Sometimes karma can be returned in this life or the next and by that reasoning it can come from a past life or this one. There are personal karma, family karma, country karma and the big one, world karma, but for now let's look at the first one, with number two making a guest-star appearance later.

We all change what we say and often what we do to fit in with other people's perception of who we should be, but is that any way to behave? By now you will have realized just how unique you are, at least I hope you have, and it is in that uniqueness that you will find the truth of who you are. Through many lifetimes you will have gathered information, bad habits and penalty points on your licence to be human! Understanding that path, that journey, is important to make assessments for your future.

So where do you begin with this? Well, have you ever seen someone and immediately felt you didn't like them or even that you loved them? This extreme reaction can indicate a link in a former life, but it doesn't have to mean unfinished business, in fact it can sometimes mean finished business and the feeling you get is a warning to stay well away and not start another karmic cycle. Of course it needn't always be about people, it's usually about emotional responses to situations and patterns that need to be either enhanced or broken. It's about bringing the positive to the fore and dealing with the not-so-great once and for all. Perhaps a look at that life I mentioned earlier would help explain this whole karma thing?

As you recall, I'm there in little more than a tea towel waiting for a battle to commence. I must admit I was feeling confident and I even remember it was a beautiful day and I said so to the soldier next to me!

I didn't see the battle, as I seemed to move beyond it and into the private rooms of a very fine young woman who I am ashamed to say was not my wife. I know – bad, isn't it? Moving swiftly on, we had what you might call an evening of celebration, and after celebrating at least twice I rose to look at the sun as it nudged its way through the shuttered windows. Then I remember looking back at the woman's beauty and leaving to return home. There I found my wife and five, yes five, children anxiously waiting for me to come back after the battle and all exuberant at my return. I embraced them one and all, noticing from my twentieth-century consciousness that one of the children was my mother in this life and another a very good friend.

Daily life went on until once more it was time to fight a battle. This time the odds for survival were a little worse than before, but off I went. The look in my family's eyes as I did so sent me off into tears at this point and it took me a few deep breaths and a lot of effort to carry on.

This time I seemed to have a lot more to wear. This was an indication of my elevation from the ranks to the role of officer, and as such I was summoned to the general's tent for a war briefing. Two senior officers were waiting there. They duly told me my duties and dismissed me. Oddly, I recognized them as two older friends of mine in this life. I noted this and moved on.

I bet you're thinking, 'This is it. Big drama, big fight and good night, toga boy.' You're wrong. Once more I proved my mettle and survived, and once more I didn't take the direct route home. Once more I slept in the arms of my occasional acquaintance, and this is where it gets interesting. I woke to hear her shuffling about and went over to her. She offered me a drink from a jug of wine that had just been brought in and, being a little thirsty, I drank deeply. Unfortunately for me, the wine was poisoned. It wasn't meant for me, I have to say, but it was poisoned anyway and that was that. It had been poisoned on the instruction of the generals and sent because the woman involved was using her charms to corrupt the governing powers.

Several relationships were revealed in that life. The two generals are now in my life and at one time or another they have been responsible for making sure I have been fed and watered. One was particularly kind when I found myself homeless and penniless; the other offered me spiritual nurturing, even to the point of allowing me the honour of sitting by him as he shuffled off this mortal coil after a horrendous illness that he bore with the greatest dignity and humour.

One of my children in that life is now one of my best friends and even though he does sometimes still treat me like his father, he has turned a corner and now advises me more than I do him.

The *femme fatale*? She and I resumed our activities for a time and although things didn't work out in the end, she too was responsible for keeping me safe when my world crumbled – a karmic debt repaid in full.

Through the past-life regression I learned that emotionally I was stronger than I thought and that I was capable of anything if I applied myself enough. I also learned I was able to stand up for myself when I needed to, but above all I discovered names, dates and places in the history books and that was the true start of my spiritual journey, even though it was to take a few more years before the whole pneumonia thing!

Oddly enough, in this life I have never been unfaithful in a relationship and to this day it's something I dislike intensely.

Through this experience I gained more questions than I did answers, but it put me firmly on a path that will only end when I do. And then another one will no doubt open up!

After several more past-life regressions and undertaking my own meditations I found a common bond in the lives I saw. That bond is what keeps me driven in the here and now. You cannot possibly know everything in life, but what you can do is know who you are and where you've come from – and in my case I'm not just talking about that little mining community in Scotland!

Case Study

Now, just to give you another example of what happens in a past-life regression, here's the story of Kate. She came to me mainly as an explorer. That wasn't her job – what I mean is she was looking for some answers and felt drawn to past-life regression. She wasn't already on a path, if you like, just looking to see where she might want to walk.

After looking at her natal chart I noticed that with Scorpio rising and her Sun and Moon in Pisces her path might be a both emotional and intense one. Not wanting to put anything into her mind before we began, I didn't mention the astrology but did use her chart after the regression to offer advice on the way ahead – a classic way of using one tool to enhance another.

Here's a pared-down transcript of her past-life regression:

DW: What are you wearing on your feet?

Kate: *Soft leather shoes, very basic.*

DW: Come up your body and tell me what else you are wearing.

Kate: *Animal skins, very loose, and I have bones and things in my hair!*

DW: What kind of bones?

Kate: *Animals, little animal things. My hair is filthy – I hate it!*

DW: Are you male or female and what age do you think you are?

Kate: *Female, aged about 48.*

DW: Are you inside or out?

Kate: *Outside a tent. I think I'm an American Indian!*

DW: OK, so tell me what's happening.

Kate: *People are coming to me for cures. I know I also deliver babies and tend to the wounded.*

DW: What would you say you were to these people?

Kate: *I'm the wise woman. The healer, I guess.*

DW: Is it a role you enjoy?

Kate: *I think it's important to uphold our ways and I tell stories to the children about animal guides and our ancestors.*

DW: Do you know what tribe you belong to?

Kate: *No. I suddenly feel very fearful and can only see blackness.*

DW: Go back to telling the children your stories.

Kate cries at this point.

DW: Why are you crying, Kate?

Kate: *They're so full of life and I'm so old.*

DW: Why should that make you feel so sad?

Kate: *I don't know.*

DW: I want you to move forward to a very important time. Go slowly and let me know when you are there.

Kate: *OK. I'm sitting on a mountainside, wrapped in furs. I have some water and a little food – not much – and I am ill, very ill.*

DW: Why are you on a mountain?

Kate: *I have been left to die. It's the tradition when one of us slows the others down and I am at the end of my life, a liability. I can't say anything because it's part of all those things I have held so dear.*

DW: How do you feel now it's happening to you?

Kate: *I feel let down by those I love, but I use the time to make peace with my soul and those who left me.*

DW: What's happening now?

Kate: *I can see a light coming towards me. It's beautiful.*

DW: Surround yourself with that light and let me know when you are completely surrounded by it.

Kate: *OK.*

DW: Is there anyone waiting for you in the light?

Kate: *No, nobody.*

DW: Look again.

Kate: *I can see my son from that life. He says he's sorry, if it were his decision he would have carried me on his own back. I tell him I understand and we hug.*

Kate cries.

Kate: *Sorry, sorry.*

DW: What are you sorry for, Kate?

Kate: *For hating him when it was my own decision in the end. I was the one who decided to show the old ways were the best ways.*

DW: What negative feelings or habits have you noticed from that life that may have carried into this one, Kate?

Kate: *I assume responsibility for everything and everyone and end up resenting it later on, sometimes taking it out on the very people I want to help and love.*

DW: I want you to see that as a colour, a shape, maybe words, and see how they are attached to you by a silver cord. Then let that cord break, let it break and allow those negative feelings to drift away. Let them go and don't look at them ever again. Now, what positive things do you want to recognize from that life?

Kate: *I do have the ability to help people with some sort of intuition I have never really admitted to and my affinity with nature is underused. When I'm in it I feel whole. I just don't get into it enough.*

DW: Are you happy to leave it there?

Kate: *Yes.*

DW: Bring your consciousness back into the room, focus on the ceiling and wiggle your fingers and toes.

There was a lot more information from Kate that was personal and a lot she could go away and research to find more proof for herself.

After a few more regressions she began to change dramatically. Now she says 'no' a lot more frequently, thereby freeing up her own time and letting people resolve their own worries where previously she would take them on, but when advice is clearly needed she gives it, based on her intuition. Her spiritual path is now more strongly linked to the world of nature and the Earth and one big thing has happened to her physical self. Having learned that she starved to death in a previous incarnation, she realized her overeating in this life was a result of that, and once she reminded her subconscious there was no need to panic any more she began to lose weight

– three stone, to be precise!

It's important to remember that Kate's subsequent visits to this life and others helped her to form a relationship with her soul as well as her inner vision, making her more adept at spotting what was right and wrong for her in this present incarnation.

Doing It Yourself

Would you like to try it? With past-life regression, there's nothing like experiencing it for yourself. There are many psychics and past-life therapists out there who will tell you what happened to you in a past life, but the whole point of the exercise is to enable that channel from your subconscious mind to your conscious mind to open up, and you won't do that by asking someone else to tell you who you were in a past life, no matter how accurate they are. That doesn't mean to say you can't visit a psychic after you have done some work on your own or been to a past-life therapist who gets you to do the work. But 'what you see and do you will remember; what you're told you will forget' – and that applies whether you are learning to use a computer or to enhance your psychic self. So the best thing to do is have a past-life regression of your own.

Finding someone who can do this for you isn't always straightforward. Ways can range from word of mouth to surfing the net, but what you must do is trust where you are and whom you are with. At the first sign of discomfort, walk away. It's sometimes a good thing to take a friend with you on your first visit. They can take notes for you, but make sure it's someone to whom you can lay your soul bare. Why don't you both have a regression and compare notes?

I'm going to take you on a journey to read the Akashic records soon. But before you start, here are a few more things you need to know about exploring your past lives.

How Will It Help Me?

You can benefit from past-life work in several areas:

- your subconscious can communicate better with your conscious mind

- you can understand your interpersonal relationships better

- your confidence can rise

- you can overcome fears and phobias

- you can eat less

- you can kick bad habits such as smoking

- you can contact your guides and angels

- you can learn to confront others more effectively.

How Will It Happen?

What people worry most about is whether they will go back or not, but put that out of your mind. You *will* go back, especially now you know how to meditate. *How* you will experience the whole thing is more what you need to think about. People's senses in a past-life regression vary. Some get the full-on Hollywood experience whilst others see colour and just 'feel' their way through it.

Think back to your meditation work. How did you see your forest? Did you hear the animals? Could you feel the temperature? What did you see? Could you taste and smell things when you were there? There is no right or wrong here, no better or worse, there's simply the way you do it, and even that changes sometimes. I am stronger with my sight and my hearing, for example, but recently taste and smell have become easier to deal with. If you see nothing at all, you may find your emotions are the key. Let them be the path that will unfold your tale and don't dismiss anything – even the smallest of details can be massively significant.

One observation that's very interesting is that sometimes even those who can usually have the full Hollywood experience can sometimes land in a past life and not see a thing – because they were blind in that life. You see how you have to trust in the process and concentrate on what's going on!

Remember that through it all you are your own judge about what's real or not. Stick to that – it's principle number one.

Also remember your Sun sign, as it will give some indication as to what sort of experience you will have. You may already have recognized that in your meditation exercises. So, Virgo, don't be too analytical. Gemini, don't be too anxious to move on. Pisces, be sure to eat and drink afterwards!

Taking the Journey

The first place you are going to be taken to is the Akashic records. Remember that's a library that contains the history of your soul. Before we go, let's just think for a moment about the difference between your soul and your personality.

Your personality is the way you get around. It's the car, if you like, and your soul is the driver. (The spirit is the satellite navigation system, by the way!) Without the personality, the soul goes nowhere and that isn't its intention. The personality has a one-life sell-by date. Once you move on, it will eventually go and your soul will shop around for a new vehicle to give it the best chance of learning and fulfilling its karma in your next life.

When you visit a past life, try to remember what that soul experience feels like. It's all too easy to get caught up in the personality stuff and whilst it is important you can learn a lot from looking at the soul. This becomes clearer when you have had a series of past-life regressions; the soul path shows itself then with more ease.

In the following exercise the Akashic records may show you more than one life. Later, when you have a full regression, they're more likely to show only one.

You already know how to meditate. Think about this as a guided visualization and remember to put white light around you. Think about your intention, get comfortable, don't have a full tummy or a rumbly one, relax and enjoy the experience, but above all keep an open mind.

 Here we go.

You find yourself in the forest. See it around you and let it build in your own time. Be sure-footed and secure as you walk along the now familiar path.

See your animal guide ahead. Is it still the same one? Follow it to the base of an oak tree. Take your time. There's no need to hurry.

As you approach the door, it opens and you enter a room at the base of the tree. It has a black-and-white chequered floor covered with herbs. Smell them as they are crushed under your feet and walk towards the back of the room, where you will see a blue flame burning on a plain altar.

Move behind the altar and towards a door at the back of the room. Allow it to open and there you will see a massive orange ball of light. Inside it there appears to be a chair. Sit on it.

The light begins to move upwards, taking you and the chair with it and surrounding you in a perfect glow. It is a protective and comforting experience.

As the orange ball takes you up into the universe, enjoy the comfort and light and the healing it offers and just relax.

When you are ready, imagine the ball of light settling into a snowy frozen landscape and then step out into a sunny day in that icy world.

Ahead you will see a path has been cleared in the snow. There appear to be words and musical symbols frozen underneath. Do you recognize any of them? Follow the path.

As you proceed you will see a massive circular building ahead of you. It is a magnificent structure with doors all the way round and steps up to them that also appear to be covered in words.

Approach the building and choose your door. Take care on those slippery steps. That's it, go towards your door.

Now look at the door you have chosen. What's it made of? Are there any carvings on it and if so, what are they?

The door will open and you will enter a corridor. Let the door close behind you and move along the corridor. As you do so, take note of any objects that decorate this hallway. These were yours in a former life and will offer some clues to your past lives.

As you reach the end of the corridor another door awaits. This will take you into the library and to your own very special book. Wait outside the door until an attendant comes to help you. Take note of who, or indeed what, they present themselves as.

Now, as the door opens, follow this guide into the library. They will lead you to a desk where your book awaits.

Sit down and feel the book. Touch it. What does it feel like? Is there a name on the front of the book? If there is, take note of it. This is your soul name and those that do see it can consider themselves very lucky. Don't tell anyone what it is, though. Sharing it is akin to giving away your pin number – it's a special name only your guides will call you by.

Now let the book open. You may see words or pictures, feel things or hear things. Remember, it's all down to you and you alone. Spend some time simply being with your book.

When you are ready, close the book and wait for your guide to take you back to the hallway exit. Thank them for their help.

Now move along your corridor once more, looking left and right at things that may have been precious to you once.

Leave the library and head towards that ball of orange light – your taxi back!

Let the light close around you, relax once more and enjoy the journey back to your tree.

Once in the room under your oak tree, step out of the orange ball, let the door close behind you and walk through the room. If you wish, it might be nice to bow at the altar in recognition of the gift of knowledge you have received.

Now leave the room, go back into your forest and follow your animal back to your starting-point. Thank them and then let the forest fade, returning your consciousness to the here and now.

Kettle on. Biscuits out.

Take some time to write down what you have experienced. Take as long as you need. More information may come to you later in the day or week. If it does, don't forget to write that down too.

When you are ready, discuss it with your friends if you are doing things that way.

You will consolidate things later when you have learned a way into a deeper mediation and an individual life. That's what we'll do now – are you ready to experience something a little deeper?

📖   Think about your intention, see that white light around you and above all be comfortable. For this session you might find it best to lie down. On the floor is fine. Put a cushion under your head and your knees if it helps.

You find yourself in the forest. See it around you and let it build in your own time. Be sure-footed and secure as you walk along the now familiar path.

See your animal guide ahead. Is it still the same one? Follow it to the base of your oak tree. Take your time. There's no need to hurry.

As you approach the door, it opens and you enter the room at the base of the tree. See the black-and-white chequered floor, smell the herbs as they are crushed under your feet and walk towards the back of the room where you will see the blue flame burning on the plain altar.

As well as the blue flame, this time you will see a brass lamp, one that looks as though Aladdin may have owned it. Pick it up. This is the lamp of memory.

With your lamp in your hand, walk behind the altar and go towards the door at the back of the room. As you approach it, watch it open.

Behind the door there's an odd mist, a fog. Don't be afraid, just walk into it and hear the door close behind you. Keep on walking.

As you walk, count backwards from ten. Ten: you feel yourself relaxing more; nine: your steps seem lighter; eight: your awareness of your surroundings changes;

seven: you feel more optimistic; six: your whole body feels lighter; five: you feel your image changing; four: the mist begins to clear a little; three: you catch glimpses of another landscape; two: your feet feel different; and one: you are through the mist.

Now trust in those feelings we mentioned earlier. What are you wearing on your feet? Come up your body and sense whether you are male or female and what age.

Do you have a name or date that comes to mind?

Are you indoors or out?

Is it warm or cold?

Are there any people around you and if there are, who are they?

Do you recognize anyone from your twenty-first-century life?

How emotional do you feel?

Where do these emotions come from?

Let your story unfold.

Allow yourself to go as far as you are comfortable with. If you don't feel that great with it all, remember all you have to do is wiggle your toes and your fingers and open your eyes.

How did that life end?

When you feel it's over, go into the light and ask to talk to anyone you want to from that life. Listen carefully to what's said to you.

What negative traits from that life do you want to leave behind? See them attached to you and sever that cord, allowing them to float off.

What positive traits are you bringing back with you? Hold onto them tightly!

Prepare to come back when you are ready.

One: go towards the door ahead of you; two: let it open and move into the mist; three: remember to carry the lamp back with you; four: your steps are getting heavier; five: you begin to become aware of noises around you; six: you begin to feel your physical body; seven: you see the door back into your oak tree ahead of you; eight: the smell of the herbs begins to fill your nostrils; nine: you're more aware of your own body; and ten: you're back in the room.

Now put your lamp back and leave. Take the path back through the forest. When you are ready, let the forest melt away and open your eyes.

This time you will have to wait a little while before moving and when you do, do it slowly.

Kettle on, biscuits open.

Now write down your experience and put in anything else that comes to you. Sometimes you will get more information for up to two days afterwards!

If you do this with a mate, you may want to give yourself at least half an hour between regressions to allow for some energy replacement. If you go first, your mate will be anxious to get on. Don't let them pressure you into it! Take your time.

Don't do this any more than once a month, as you need time to assimilate what you have learned and to think about how it affects your life now. If you can, why not research the life and see what you can find out? Proof often comes in the smallest of ways.

Changing the Outcome

Once you have had your past-life regression, you can go back and change the outcome if you wish – press the cosmic rewind button, if you like!

What would be the benefits of this? A lot of psychic development is simply about changing the way your subconscious remembers events. So by going back and consciously putting in a different ending you are saying you no longer accept the debris left over from a previous incarnation and want to move on and up!

Here's an example. A friend of mine was having problems with a man she knew she had been with in a former life. They weren't major problems – he was just dragging his heels a bit on the commitment front. In the former life she had sat around waiting for him, often refusing things that would have been good for her in order to make him happy, until one day she was old and bored out of her mind whilst he was off doing what he wanted and inevitably he died, leaving her even more bored.

Going back into that life, she chose a point in time where an offer to go to university had come her way and this time she took it. This part of the regression moved more quickly than the first and she really had to let go and allow her own intuition to take over at this point. It did, with a new story unfolding in front of her eyes. Initially, her new decision shocked this man in her former life, but he soon got used to it and their relationship became one with more balance. Whilst he still died at the same time, the woman she was had a full and happier life both before and after his demise. Often solutions like these can be a bit of a shock and some people fight them. Try not to and you too will have great results.

Back in the twenty-first century, things began to change as my friend became less focused on the big white frock and the man responded by being more comfortable around her. It took time – this isn't a five-minute wonder – but their relationship changed and became more balanced and I'm happy to say they are now married and are planning their first child soon. This is a perfect example of just how enhancing your psychic skills can have a positive effect on your life.

Consolidation

What have you learned about yourself and your abilities?

In your journal you should now have at least two past-life visits, one from the Akashic records and one more in-depth one. Is there a common thread?

What areas are they suggesting you look at and will you acknowledge them? Remember to include what you have already learned about yourself. It's around now that you should begin to form a much stronger link with your soul, that part of you that knows the bigger plan.

Go back to your past lives. How did you experience them? Were they all about hearing, seeing or tasting? Did you feel anything or did you smell any smells?

What about your emotions?

Whom did you see from your present life and what were those past relationships telling you about them? Are you travelling with the same people?

Has a search on the internet or in your local library come up with any confirmation?

Write it all down, it will be useful!

CHAPTER 6

GUIDES

There is a chance that even in the early stages of your development you will be introduced to a spirit guide, a teacher if you like. You will have a principal guide who will have an interest in your development from birth to death. They normally present themselves when you are ready to see them and not before. Sometimes they come through in past-life work simply because you are more likely to be dealing with soul work then and not personality issues. This is what really interests this level of guide. They want you to do well and are willing to help, if you ask. That's the one thing people forget to do! But without that permission nobody in the spiritual realms can do a thing. They can suggest, they can point, but unless you ask they won't do as much as they are capable of. In addition to this guide you are likely to have teachers who move in and out of your life according to where you are.

One of my most profound awakening moments happened around a guide. Only a few months after I had begun to study astrology and the Qabala, a friend of mine called Mo came to the house. Mo is a psychic, and a very good one at that. She told me that a guide who had been with me for many years was leaving and wished to say goodbye, but she would like to do it through a meditation. I agreed and duly sat down. Guided by Mo, I went to meet the guide in question.

Just for a change I got very emotional and cried as my third eye showed me the beauty of my guide's light and my heart chakra opened up to give and receive the love around her. She kissed me on my cheek – I actually physically felt it – and walked away without looking back. Bereft, I moped around the house for days. This guide had been with me for 32 years and I missed her. I later found out she had left because her job was done. She had been there to guide me to the moment of my awakening and like any good teacher she recognized the moment to leave.

Then one night I woke up and there she was, manifest at the end of my bed smiling at me and reminding me she would always know what I was up to. Then, as quickly as she had appeared, she was gone.

Trust

When you arrive at the end of your past-life regression you may sense the presence of your own guide. Alternatively, you may not. For me there is only one rule when it comes to guides, and that's to trust in what *you* see rather than worry about what others say – a common theme, I feel. When I first met my own guide I was a little worried by the fact that he was a Native American, but that was just because I'd been listening to people who had opened their throat chakra before their crown and heart!

Throughout your development, never be embarrassed about saying what you see. It may not mean anything to anyone else – they may even think it enhances their life to make you sound silly – but the truth is the truth. Have confidence in that and in yourself.

So why the fancy dress? Well, if your guide was a

plumber, what would that tell you about them? Not a lot. Which is why they present as Native Americans, gentle spirited ladies in flowing gowns, Merlin-like old men etc., etc. That way you have more of a sense of who they are and what they are likely to bring to you. Merlin types will probably steer you in the direction of Wicca or earth magik, graceful ladies tend to be about peace, tranquillity and calming of the spirit, and Native Americans are linked to the cycles of life among many other things.

Often a guide will hide their face from you. If they do, don't ask for it to be revealed. They will do that in their own time.

Meeting their guide is something people get really hot under the collar over. Relax! Remember, too, that you can never go to your guide, they can only come to you, and they won't do that until you are ready. There really is no harm, though, in making known your intention to meet them. Here's a meditation to help you on your way.

📖 Prepare to meditate.

The level you will be raising yourself to here requires a little more from you in the way of set-up, so before you begin I want you to imagine that before you is a pillar of sparkling blue and ultraviolet light, behind you is a pillar of water that is bluer than you have ever seen, to your right is a pillar of fire and to your left a pillar of stone and wood.

Know that this is the protection of the angelic forces of Raphael for Air, Michael for Fire, Gabriel for Water and Uriel for Earth and they will be with you on your journey.

Now go to your forest and wander.

Eventually you find a clearing and in it you see a pool of water. Go and sit by that pool. Feel relaxed and comfortable. Notice any animals that pass by.

Look to your right and you will see a figure. There's no need to be afraid. It might only be a change in the light perhaps, but you will notice something.

Give this light time to change shape, to show itself. Who is it?

Ask if this person is your guide. If you hear that it is, ask them for a name. You may not get one first time. Don't worry, this sometimes takes a while.

Now ask any questions you might have.

Your guide will give you a gift and depart. Thank them for their presence.

Sit by the pool and think about what you have seen.

When you are ready, make your way back through the forest.

Return your consciousness back into the room.

This time tea is not enough – make sure you have toast or something more substantial!

Write down and/or discuss what you have seen.

Know that you can contact your guide whenever you need to. Don't be worried about asking for help – that is what they are there for. You can also be aware when they are around you.

Doorkeepers

These are similar to guides, but their sole, or should that be soul, purpose is to protect you from any negative influences or thoughts that could distract you. They often present themselves as warriors. Mine shows himself as an executioner, with axe and all! Doorkeepers stand at your crown chakra and defend your right to your own thoughts as opposed to those of others.

If you would like to meet your doorkeeper, use the same meditation as the one for meeting your guide and don't be put off by their ferocity. Remember, they are on your side.

When you begin to do psychic work, simply ask them to stand by your side and then forget about them, let them get on with it.

Your Ego

One of the things you have to do on your path to psychic development is not only get to know your guide but also your ego. So, what is that exactly? We all know that the term 'egotistical' is used to describe someone who is too big for their boots! Step away from that judgement and think of it this way – we all have an ego. It's that part of us that wants to be something we aren't and to have all those things we don't have!

Your ego hinders you when it effectively blanks out the reality of a situation. It will also put you in a defensive or aggressive position to get what you think you want rather than what you actually do want.

Oddly enough, it is probably your ego that has brought

you this far, but it will have done its job by now and if you continue to use it, there will be fireworks when it realizes that it wants things that you no longer find important! Mine was a little upset when it realized the luxury yacht was probably a step too far.

When you decide you no longer want to work from your ego but want to work from your soul instead, you are ready to move forward. So what's the difference? Like any good teacher, I am not going tell you. If you can't feel the shift, you haven't made it!

Prepare to meditate with the intention of meeting your ego.

Imagine you are in your forest. See it, feel it, sense it around you.

Beneath an ancient oak you see a doorway. It appears to be built into the very wood itself. Go through the door.

You enter the room with the altar with the blue flame burning on it. This time a magician is standing by it. (Think Merlin here, not David Blaine.)

As you approach the altar, he asks you if you are ready to see your ego, to set it free, to embrace life without the judgements it can place on you.

Reply that you are and move towards him.

He asks you to move towards the back of the room where you see a curtain with your image on it. Move through that curtain and onto a path strewn with yellow and blue flowers.

Follow the path at your leisure until you see someone approaching in the distance. It looks like, it can't be, yes it is — it's you.

Look at yourself with the eyes of someone meeting you for the first time. What do you project, what do you feel about yourself, how do you react to meeting a stranger? See yourself as others see you.

Talk to your ego and ask all those questions you want to ask yourself when you do something that you simply know is not really you!

Spend some time with your ego, then say thank you. Without your ego you would not be here.

Now let it return to where it came from down that beautiful path.

Walk back through the curtain to the room beneath the tree. Has anything changed in the room?

Find your magician and briefly thank him and leave.

Walk into your forest and when you are ready, bring your consciousness back into the room.

Pop the kettle on and write down your experience and discuss it with your friends if appropriate.

So is ego a bad thing?

There you have it. Think about what you have uncovered here – or should that be whom? You have met beings who are important to you and you have probably met one that's beginning to grow on you more than most – the real you!

Consolidation

To consolidate this chapter, why don't you go for a walk and see if you can link in with your guide. Let them walk beside you and imagine a conversation between the two of you. This is best done in your head, as talking to yourself is still one of those things that gets you noticed for all the wrong reasons! Pick somewhere beautiful, somewhere that will fill your heart and theirs.

Now think about what you no longer need in your life, what your ego can do without and you are happy to let go of.

In your journal write down your experiences and anything that comes to you as you do so. Remember that as you write in this precious journal you're still linked to your sub-conscious and any thoughts are important.

CHAPTER 7

THE TAROT

There are as many myths surrounding the Tarot as there are decks themselves. You will hear various ideas, from the cards being a device to bury esoteric teaching right through to just a game played by aristocrats. For our purposes they are a window into your subconscious.

The deck itself is made up of 22 Major Arcana cards and 56 Minor Arcana ones. The Major Arcana give you bigger messages; they suggest long-term changes and areas you really have to concentrate on. The 56 Minor Arcana suggest day-to-day, more earthly challenges you may have to deal with. The Minor Arcana are split into four suits, just like playing cards. Each suit has 14 cards in it – ace to ten and four court cards, namely the Knight (or King), the Queen, Prince (Knight in some decks) and Princess (or Page). They are then split into the suits of Wands, which represent Fire, Swords, which represent Air, Cups, which represent Water, and Disks, which represent Earth. We'll talk more about the elements and the cards themselves later on.

You don't have to be given your first Tarot deck – that's another myth. You can go out and buy it if you like. I use the Thoth deck – you can use whichever one you want!

If you are buying a deck, though, be guided by your intuition. The cards work through images, and images are the language of your intuition and psychic mind. It's through the plethora of symbols, and in the case of the Thoth deck astrological references as well, that you will discover more about your own path and how to access the ancient wisdom the Tarot contains. The 78 cards can make you smile as time and time again the same things are suggested to you, as I have found out!

I cannot stress enough how important the images are when using the Tarot – and it's your own interpretation of them that counts. One of the best bits of advice I ever got with the Tarot was to read the books on it then give them away. If you constantly refer to them, you have missed the point!

During my time learning the Qabala the cards were to become very familiar to me. Part of the structure of the Qabala allows for a deeper understanding of the cards. That takes many years, but you don't have to take years to use the cards; you can pick a pack up today and get something from it immediately.

When I was given my first deck it was suggested that I take the cards with me into a meditation and ask for them to be linked to my subconscious. You too can do this by simply holding your cards during a meditation and asking for that link. This time there's no help from me – you can do this yourself. Make it short, but do it the way you want to do it. And don't forget your intention. In this case it's to form a relationship with your cards.

Before we meet the characters and influences involved with the cards it may be a good thing to know how to handle them. I am a little superstitious with my cards and like to keep them wrapped in a piece of black silk and in a lovely box. I'm not sure if it is superstition or a show of respect for their wisdom; either way, it makes it special when I unwrap them and in a way it sends a signal to my own subconscious to really wake up, it has work to do! I also drop some essential oil onto the silk now and again to keep the cards clean and smelling lovely. I love to use geranium oil for this as it smells sweet and has an air of calm about it. You might want to come up with your own ritual. Ritual is good – it switches you on and somehow connects you to the cards in a way that you won't have if you simply pick them up and start working.

Questions and Answers

Most of us think of the cards as an oracle, a way to have our questions answered, and they will do that, or should that be you do it with their assistance?

You can ask questions out loud or you can ask in your own head. Both ways are fine. Just be clear about your intention.

Simple 'yes' and 'no' questions don't work very well with the Tarot and the cards won't tell you what to do either. They will, however, suggest an outcome if you choose a particular route. So don't say 'Should I apply for this job?' but 'What will happen if I apply for this job?'

Choosing the Cards

There are various ways of laying the cards out according to the question you want an answer to. We'll come to those later, but first it's a good thing to shuffle the deck! Hold the cards, cut them, shuffle them. Handling them is the key, it puts your energy around the cards, and as you shuffle just think about your question once to reinforce it and then let your intuition take over. There is nothing wrong with some-one else choosing your cards for you, by the way. There are times when that just feels appropriate or perhaps distance makes it the only practical way.

When the cards are good and mixed up, put them back into a neat pile and hold them sticking out from your belly button. This puts them firmly in your aura. It always makes me feel really connected to the cards.

Now run the fingers of your left hand (that's your intu-itive side, whether you are right- or left-handed) up and down the cards and take one out when you feel guided.

Take as many cards as you need for your chosen layout, keeping them in order. Remember to lay them out in the order that you chose them. Mixing up the order won't give you an accurate reading.

Now put them face down the way you want to read them – card one in position one, card two in position two, and so on.

Reading the Cards

Some people prefer to turn over one card at a time. Personally, I like to see the whole lot, as simple things like the dominant colour in the lay can bring something to me or perhaps there are lots of nines or court cards – something that could be significant to the whole scheme of things. You decide how you prefer to turn the cards – it's your Tarot.

Upside-down cards often have a negative interpretation thrust on them. I don't bother which way up the cards are. There's positive and negative in every card and it's up to you which interpretation you are drawn to. Just go with it.

Read each card in relation to its position in your chosen

lay, but remember to relate it to the card ahead and the one behind as well. This is a flow of information, not an isolated message, and at the end of the lay you should have been taken on a journey by your psychic self, a journey through your subconscious.

Frequently Asked Questions

What can I ask and is anything forbidden?

Apart from avoiding 'yes' and 'no' questions, you can ask anything you like. Nothing is forbidden. Your own moral judgement will guide you!

How can people with no knowledge of the cards pull the right cards for themselves?

Remember you're dealing with the subconscious. It knows everything and it will access the right information – perhaps not just about the person drawing the cards, but about the person reading them as well.

Can I really read my own cards?

Staying objective isn't easy, but when it comes to your psychic development you will usually find the cards are clear. If you use them for personality issues such as love, money and career, that can be difficult and you do have to work hard at detaching what you want to see from what's actually being said. That takes a long, long time, as I have found out.

Should I be scared of the cards?

Are you scared of postcards? Just like them, Tarot cards are bits of cardboard with pictures on them. They help you access your own subconscious and nothing in that will scare you!

The myths surrounding the Tarot can be off-putting, but they were probably simply meant to stop people accessing something that handed power back to them. Some people prefer others not to ask questions and to just do what they're told!

How do you know which symbol or meaning to use?

You trust your intuition and let your eye be drawn to what your subconscious is showing you. Go with what you see. It's a bit like a cosmic game of *Catch-phrase* – say what you see.

If a card comes out more than once, is it especially important?

The card itself isn't important, it's the message that's being reinforced – usually because you're not listening!

How far ahead will the cards work if used for prediction?

Think weeks rather than months, up to about eight weeks in fact, but always remember, if the cards suggest change and you do nothing, nothing will change. Never blame the cards for lack of action in your life.

Should I invest in a headscarf and earrings?

The cards aren't about fortune-telling, they are about your soul, about your development as a spiritual being, and as such they should be used to show you how you can help yourself rather than whether you're going to meet someone special down the pub tonight.

Can I overdo it?

Yes, you can, and I have. I take a card every day as part of my meditation routine, but I don't live by it and when I do a full lay I only do it as part of a process, I don't make it the only tool for deciding my way ahead. If you find yourself consulting the Tarot to decide what to have for your tea, you might need to put the cards away for a while!

Can I read for friends?

If you like. It's a good way to practise, but remember you may see things you don't want to comment on. Make sure if you do read for friends you only do it when both of you are sober. This is no party trick and shouldn't be treated as such.

Is distance a problem?

You can read for someone at a distance and they can read for you. Just make sure you take some time to think about them and get a link. Without it, you might as well be sitting playing patience.

◆◆◆◆

Are you ready to meet the team?

The Major Arcana

As we go through the cards, take your deck out and have a look at each card. Don't hurry this process. Make some notes about how each card makes you feel and what the colour or symbols mean to you. I cannot go into each and every meaning for each and every card here, but I'll give you enough information to get to grips with the Tarot. Later I'll give you a meditation process which is a very powerful method of getting to know the characters of the Major Arcana up close and personal – something I loved during my own development.

The Fool

- Number: 0

- Nature: A search for change, a leap of faith.

- Aim: To start a new cycle.

- Strength: A positive outlook, a new journey.

- Weakness: Irresponsibility, daydreams never coming true, lack of action.

This character is often seen stepping out onto a path or even about to disappear over a cliff! This can be seen as having faith he will be caught, but if you feel this card isn't favourable in a lay, it may be a warning not to be foolhardy. Over the Fool's shoulder or around him will be everything he needs for his journey, suggesting that the reader too has everything they need to embark upon the route ahead. Sometimes a dog is seen at his side, representing instinct.

Whenever I see this card in my lay I get very excited, as it usually means new things are on the horizon. Although I might have to let go of something I'm attached to, I always feel things are a little brighter for seeing the Fool.

The Magus *(The Magician)*

- Number: I

- Nature: Can do!

- Aim: To become aware of all you are capable of.

- Strength: Action, energy and ability.

- Weakness: Ego, misuse of information, sometimes dangerous gossip.

As with all good magicians, the Magus has surrounded himself with the tools of his trade. The wand, sword, cup and disk show he is master of the elements of Fire, Air, Water and Earth, meaning he can manifest whatever he wants through the proper use of his talents. Activity is indicated here. You will have the chance to get on and do things, and do things you must. Mischief can also be shown. Usually it means someone who says a little more than they ought to at a time that's not appropriate, but they will inevitably talk their way out of it!

For me, this card is special. It's Mercury, the winged messenger of the gods, and he usually says things are on their way. So when you see this card, listen carefully, keep your eyes wide open and trust what you see and hear – but check the facts before acting!

The High Priestess

- Number: II

- Nature: Intuition, a gentle whisper guiding you.

- Aim: To listen to your inner self, to allow guides to help you.

- Strength: Spiritual wisdom, tolerance and of course intuition.

- Weakness: Escapism, fantasy, moodiness and addiction.

The key to understanding the High Priestess is the veil that surrounds her. Now you see her, now you don't. She exists between the two worlds, between the conscious and subconscious, dipping in and out as she sees fit. She also moves between telling the truth and telling anything but, making this card one where your own intuition must be in full flow – funny that!

In the Thoth deck the camel at the base of the card always reminds me to hold out for what I want and the clear quartz crystals surrounding the priestess remind me to be sure about what I want! This card means divine guidance and a helping hand, but it can also warn me to make sure someone is what they say they are. If I have been overdoing things with the Tarot, this card often falls from the deck. It's one of two cards that I take to mean, 'Enough, put them away and get on with other things!'

The Empress

- Number: III

- Nature: Devotion and motherhood, female forces.

- Aim: To give birth to an idea, to bring forth a harvest.

- Strength: Nurturing, love, trust, abundance and contentment.

- Weakness: Greed, envy, rigidity and over-concern with the physical.

Sitting on her throne, the Empress looks in control in every way. She is normally surrounded by images of nature, showing her affinity with the Earth and suggesting abundance.

Femininity is the key to her success and she uses all those nurturing gifts to bring what she wants into her life. She recognizes that some old ways must die back to make way for the new and she sometimes has the Moon alongside her to show the cycle of life and death, the ebb and flow of the universe.

For me, she symbolizes all these things, but can also describe a physical pregnancy if that's appropriate in the reading. For men, she tells of a need to be more in touch with their feelings and not to be afraid to be the one who nurtures. Generally, when I see her I am warmed to know things are about to take a turn for the better, to move from winter to spring.

The Emperor

- Number: IV

- Nature: Rulership, control and leadership.

- Aim: To do the right thing, to observe the rules.

- Strength: Creativity, action, objective responsibility and the positive force of change.

- Weakness: Dictatorship, inflexibility, harsh speech, action without intuition.

This very strong figure is associated with Aries and all the Arian traits apply here. He is of course on his throne, telling everyone he is in charge, and the rams, another symbol for

Aries, show his virility and ability to lead. He wants to see some courage in the face of adversity and reckons the only way to have that is to speak up rather than lurk in the shadows, muttering and backbiting. He may have a point! For women, this card can suggest taking on a more active role or perhaps remind them of their own creativity and the need to be assertive.

To me, this card means action stations. It says it is a time to get on with things rather than sit around and wait for them to happen.

The Hierophant

- Number: V

- Nature: The search for hidden truth, a spiritual guide.

- Aim: To achieve enlightenment from the inside out.

- Strength: A search for the truth regardless of the opinions of others. Faith.

- Weakness: Narrow-mindedness, spiritual egotism and presumption.

Here we meet our spiritual teacher. Sometimes this card can actually represent a physical person coming into your life to help with your teaching as well as a new spirit guide. The Hierophant appears very much in control of himself and usually his hands are open to show his willingness to share. Interestingly, he often has the index and middle finger together on his left hand, forming horns. This reminds us of the illusions we may encounter in the search for enlightenment.

I love this card, he is very special to me, and when I see him he reminds me to keep searching and to follow my own path regardless of those who want to impose too many rules!

The Lovers

- Number: VI

- Nature: Union, marriage, opposites attracting.

- Aim: To become one.

- Strength: A choice made from the depths of your heart, a courageous decision.

- Weakness: Indecisiveness, love as a fantasy, the sacrifice of self for another.

The meaning of this card may seem obvious, and in some cases it is, but what if it comes up when the question is about something unrelated to love – career, for example? Here the duality of the card comes into play and suggests a choice has to be made. It won't tell you what that choice is; it will, however, show the answer lies within you and to find it all you have to do is to be emotionally honest with yourself. The people in this card represent the severing of one into two, so what is needed to become whole again?

For me, this card is always welcome when the question is about love, as it indicates there is a strong bond, but does it mean physical love? That all depends on the cards around it and on its position. When the reading isn't about love, I take the Lovers as a sign that I should look more deeply into what's happening and find my own solutions, because I already know the answer I am seeking.

The Chariot

- Number: VII

- Nature: Daring, adventure, taking up the reins.

- Aim: To find the Holy Grail.

- Strength: Moving forward, getting on with the task in hand, success.

- Weakness: Authority overcoming compassion, over-riding obstacles.

The charioteer can't see where he is going and trusts in the guidance of the animals pulling his chariot, a symbol of course of using intuition and allowing things to unfold in their own time. This card says, 'I have thought this through and now I am off to meet my future.'

The Chariot means so many things to me and a lot depends on where it is in a lay, but among the meanings are: career decisions need to be made and acted on, listen to your soul, a man in uniform is in or about to come into your life and, last but by no means least, don't forget to switch the iron off before you go out. Not really – that last one was just checking you're still awake!

Adjustment *(Sometimes called Justice)*

- Number: VIII

- Nature: Harmony through seeing reality.

- Aim: To take responsibility for yourself and your actions.

- Strength: Objectivity, balance, fairness, justice.

- Weakness: Self-righteousness.

On tiptoes, blindfolded, holding the scales of justice, Maat, goddess of justice, waits to weigh your heart against a feather to see if it's light enough to allow you to enter the kingdom of heaven. You'll get what you deserve!

The organization I trained with bears the name of this Egyptian goddess, so for me this is a very special card. Maat represents fairness and eternal balance. What you sow, you reap – no more, no less. She also speaks of karma and how for every action there is an equal and opposite reaction. Her scales are not static but constantly balancing things out. When you see this card, a judgement may have to be made, but it should be made without bias.

The Hermit

- Number: IX

- Nature: Retreat, solitude, a time for reflection.

- Aim: To seek truth and knowledge, to find what you want through silence.

- Strength: Wisdom, enlightenment, maturity.

- Weakness: Hostility towards life in general, the grumpy old man/woman syndrome!

The Hermit turns away from the world towards his task of seeking knowledge and wisdom. That doesn't mean he hasn't experienced life in the big wide world but shows he has seen enough and now seeks another sort of experience. The light he carries isn't so much about showing him where he is going as showing us where he has been and illuminating a path should we wish to follow.

Again, this is one of my favourite cards. Whenever it appears, it suggests that it may be a good idea to get some time on your own to think things through. A spa is just fine for this – you don't have wear a hair shirt and sit on a mountaintop. I get some of my best ideas when I'm covered in Manuka honey and being pummelled by a hard-handed therapist!

Fortune *(Sometimes called the Wheel of Fortune)*

- Number: X

- Nature: Growth and decay, to everything there is a season.

- Aim: To accept the cycles of life and know how to use them.

- Strength: Good luck, good karma, happy coincidence.

- Weakness: Bad luck, a turn for the worse.

The obvious symbol here is the wheel. As it turns, you are either at the top or the bottom and your luck runs appropriately, but how do you know where you are? Unless you keep your eyes wide open you don't and therefore you may be out of synch with fortune. When this card appears, let yourself be guided by fate and the circumstances around you.

For me, this card is always exciting. It tends to indicate an adventure ahead and although that may mean some risks, there could be some good things to come as well. If the card is negatively placed, the idea is to lie low until things calm down, thereby minimizing the risks.

The Fortune card also indicates destiny. Use the cards around it to gain a clearer idea of where that lies.

Lust *(Sometimes called Strength)*

- Number: XI

- Nature: Charisma, creativity, energy.

- Aim: To enjoy life, to embrace all it has to offer.

- Strength: Strength, power and positive response.

- Weakness: Weakness, lack of direction, suppression of life force.

The lion seems the focal point of this card – after all, aren't lions strong? But it's the woman on the lion's back you need to be looking at. She has tamed this beast and that's where the true meaning of the card lies – in the ability to take control of life and to live it!

For me this card usually suggests someone needs to seize the moment and forget about the 'woulda, shoulda, coulda' put on them by other people. They should just do what they know to be right for them, what makes them smile. Instinct is also indicated here. Not to be confused with intuition, instinct is of the moment rather than a feeling that grows. When this card appears, it needs to be cultivated.

The Hanged Man

- Number: XII

- Nature: Sacrifice, accepting fate, devotion to a cause.

- Aim: To gain wisdom through adversity, to seek deliverance.

- Strength: Changing behaviour, overcoming negative character traits.

- Weakness: Self-sacrifice for no real reason, a refusal to act to release yourself.

Here is one of those cards people always get their pants in a panic over, no matter how many times you say there's good and bad in every card. But there's no real cause for it! The trick with the Hanged Man is to know that the man in question can get out of his dilemma any time he wants by simply releasing himself from old and outdated conditions. By seeing that there is another way to do things, he needn't suffer at all.

When I see this card I try to think how I can tackle something differently, because it's clear that continuing on the path I'm on won't produce much. Taking a new view of things will bring a freshness that will beget positive experiences.

Death

- Number: XIII

- Nature: Death and rebirth.

- Aim: To transform, like a caterpillar into a butterfly.

- Strength: Allowing room for new growth.

- Weakness: Fear, especially of death and letting go.

If the wheat in the fields didn't die, you wouldn't eat and next year's crop wouldn't grow, so your children wouldn't eat. Life and death, that cycle is perhaps the greatest one of all and the one a lot of us choose to ignore out of fear. So this is once more a negative card in some people's perception, but imagine if you are reading for someone who is in a negative relationship, one that's damaging them, and this card comes out followed by the Lovers. Wouldn't that mean the start of something better? So Death is not a negative card at all, it's one that says something is ending and it's right that it should come to an end. Most Tarot readers I know welcome this card, as it usually signifies the end of a stagnant period.

Art *(Sometimes called Temperance)*

- Number: XIV

- Nature: Emulsification, the bringing together of things that may not usually mix.

- Aim: To seek the final ingredient, the one that makes the whole thing work.

- Strength: Having everything in the right proportion, thereby creating harmony and contentment.

- Weakness: Getting the mix wrong, overdoing things on one side or another.

In the Thoth deck the figure on the Temperance card stands over a large cooking pot, adding the ingredients that will help everything to reach a fulfilling conclusion. She is surrounded by opposites, showing that nothing is impossible and with the right conditions opposites can not only attract but also work well together.

Art is one of those cards that always has the same meaning for me. It speaks of finding the missing link, the thing that's usually right in front of your nose. If you pull this card, try to think about what's working rather than what's missing, then the obvious will stand out.

The Devil

- Number: XV

- Nature: The power of illusion and persuasion. Lust for power.

- Aim: To encounter your shadow side, to confront your self.

- Strength: Seeing the whole truth of who you are and what you are capable of.

- Weakness: Being wrapped up in illusion, darkness, hysteria.

Here's another of those cards that can make some people go silly, which is fitting, as negative illusion is just what this one's about. If you look at the goat's face you will see a smile on it. It's a smile that says, 'Look at these idiots doing what I tell them just because they're too stupid to say what they really think and feel.' Got the message yet?

For me, this card speaks of a need to be more self-assured and not depend on the approval of others before making choices. This isn't the same as not caring for others' opinions or circumstances, it simply means you recognize you can make decisions and accept the consequences of those actions – you are all grown up.

The Tower

- Number: XVI

- Nature: The destruction of old structures that no longer serve you.

- Aim: To find truth and enlightenment out of the blue.

- Strength: Working through a time of major change. A change for the better.

- Weakness: Changing things for the sake of it or, worse still, just for the hell of it.

We all like to feel secure, but sometimes the walls we build to protect ourselves and perhaps to keep some people out end up keeping us in and away from experiencing life. In this card you see a tower, usually a strong building, being struck by lightning and crumbling. This suggests that no matter how strong and how high you build something, it can take just one event, one bolt from the blue, to send it tumbling down.

This card speaks to me of just that – an impending event that hasn't been sent to bring turmoil (but it might), but to make you realize you are too detached from a situation and that without your involvement things are going to get a whole lot worse. So when you draw the Tower, don't shrink away from conflict. This is a 'sleeves rolled up and get stuck in' card.

The Star

- Number: XVII

- Nature: Living in the moment, listening in the moment.

- Aim: To gain insight.

- Strength: Hope, remaining focused on what is possible.

- Weakness: Denying the truth. Being led into illusion.

Here we have a direct link to higher knowledge. The figure on the card is likened to Pandora, who in the fable opened the box containing all the world's worries, but right at the bottom found hope. Forming a link between heaven and Earth, the woman on the card pours divine light between the two, often symbolized as water.

When I see this card it tells me higher guides are there and information is available if only I will take the time to reach out for it. It also tells of maintaining hope, of staying positive, and reminds me that I'm on the right path even if things can sometimes make me feel that I'm anything but.

Dreams are also important when you see this card. Pay attention to yours and write them down when you remember them.

The Moon

- Number: XVIII

- Nature: The subconscious, the journey into your own underworld.

- Aim: To encounter, confront and face your fears.

- Strength: Intuitive knowledge.

- Weakness: Illusion, hysteria, addiction and unrealistic fears.

The Moon rules your subconscious. She is one of our oldest symbols and our Earth's constant companion, reminding us of our animal side every night as her waxing and waning affect our emotions and our moods. The Tarot card shows wolves guarding the doorway to the subconscious. Are you brave enough to walk past them, knowing you have every right to see what lies beyond? You should know that as soon as night falls, light is on its way. This is the cycle of our outer world and our inner one.

When I see this beautiful card I am reminded that fear is only an illusion and we really do have nothing to fear but fear itself. It tells of using your subconscious to remember when you have faced worse and come out smiling and to know that you are strong. For me, it also suggests acting on my emotions rather than suppressing them.

The Sun

- Number: XIX

- Nature: A move into the light.

- Aim: To come to terms with the darkness and introduce the light.

- Strength: Warmth, fresh growth, big-heartedness, confidence.

- Weakness: Smugness, an inflated ego and a superiority complex.

Where would we be without the Sun, the giver of life and something to smile about when you wake up and see it shining through the window on your wedding day? The children dancing on the card remind us to embrace life like a child, to expect nothing and to wonder at everything we do get. (Bear in mind the cards were made centuries ago!) This card is about that joy of creation, of things growing and being warmed by the Sun, of making something positive happen just by sheer will.

For me, this is the cosmic healer, the card that says, 'There, there, everything will be all right in the end.' But don't be fooled into thinking all you need to do is sit back and wait. That's a common misconception with this card. You still need to put the effort in, but with the Sun behind you the rewards are doubled!

The Aeon *(Sometimes called Judgement)*

- Number: XX

- Nature: Renewal, awakening, birth,

- Aim: To create heaven on Earth.

- Strength: Recognizing coincidence, recalling past-life memories, transformation.

- Weakness: Falsehood, greed for power.

Time is changing all the time! And this card reminds us that time is itself an illusion. It brings up all sorts of questions about what the future is and whether it is set in stone or can be changed. It reminds us that not all things are as cut and dried as some would have you think. If you draw this card, it would be wise to consider whether someone is trying to manipulate you for their own ends. It also suggests you look at circumstances in your life that seem to be guiding you along one particular path or another. Seeing them clearly will help you achieve your goals more quickly.

For me, the fact that the main character on this card has her fingers over her lip, suggesting silence, tells me to say nothing and allow others to show themselves in their full glory – or not! The bent-over figure also suggests that you may be bending over backwards to please others whilst ignoring your own needs.

The Universe

- Number: XXI

- Nature: Completion.

- Aim: To become whole.

- Strength: Resolution of events and karma.

- Weakness: Going nowhere fast.

The hermaphrodite on this card makes it neither male nor female. It's ying and yang, the perfect combination of all things masculine and feminine. The circles formed around the figure tell of beginnings and endings, of doors closing and opening – which is it for you? Hard work comes to successful conclusions when this card appears and as long as you maintain direction that will most certainly be the case.

When I see this card I am heartened to know that a project is coming to a close or another one is about to come into my life. Of course the position of the card and the cards surrounding it will affect the outcome, as will the question itself, but I almost always see this card as positive.

Just How Do You Remember All That?!

Before taking a look at the Minor Arcana, it might be good to take a break from all this mental stuff and do something more intuitive, something that will help you understand the Major Arcana better.

This meditation is going to take you into each card. Clearly time may be an issue here and you probably won't be able to look at them all. What I suggest you do is use this meditation to understand the cards you don't immediately understand. That way, it needn't be a long drawn-out thing. When I did it, it was ten minutes – and ten minutes well spent!

📖 Take a card and hold it in your hand.

Stare at it, noticing its colour, the image on it, all the tiny details…

Now close your eyes and imagine the card is still in front of you. Enlarge it until it is life-size and resembles a door rather than a card.

When you are ready, open the door and walk through into the space belonging to the card you have chosen. There you will find the characters from the card waiting for you.

Talk to them, find out what they are all about, listen to their story and laugh, cry, love and live with them.

You will know when it's time to leave. Don't overstay your welcome. Close the door and bring your awareness back to the room.

Great, isn't it? Like Disney without the air fare.

Write down what you have learned and remember that's now in your subconscious, ready to use when it's ready to be used.

The Minor Arcana

And so on to the Minor Arcana, the cards that deal with many of our day-to-day concerns and highlight details we might otherwise miss. These can also be timing cards – the numbers can represent days, weeks or months until an event. If you want to know when something is going to happen, remember to mention that in your question.

Both the positive and the negative sides of the cards are given here, but even the negative is a good thing, as it can show what needs to go. Just remember these keywords are not the only ones. As always, get to know your own cards. Let them talk to you. If you disagree with any of the words or meanings listed here, go with what you get, but be consistent. For example, the Two of Disks traditionally means change, but for me when it comes up in a reading it raises concerns over the health of someone older. I know I'm probably beginning to sound like a parrot with the trust and intuition thing, but if that's what it takes, cover me in feathers and call me Polly!

Wands

Wands symbolize energy. They come from the element of Fire. Are you going to be a slow burner or will you have an initial rush and fizzle out before the game is over? We'll see! Action and creativity are this suit's blessings.

- Ace: Energy, passion, creativity and courage. Arrogance and destruction.

- Two: Assertiveness, ruling the roost, action. Devastation.

- Three: A new beginning, having confidence in your actions. Seeking attention.

- Four: Completion, order and timing. Over-extending yourself.

- Five: Proving your abilities through adversity. Reckless actions.

- Six: Joy, victory, triumph, celebration. Egotism and pre-sumptuousness.

- Seven: Courage, a fighting spirit, having a backbone. Being indecisive, hesitant.

- Eight: Communication, knowledge, flexibility. Haste, superficiality.

- Nine: Spiritual truth and understanding, being on course. Being off course.

- Ten: Righteousness, justice and growth. Authority-figure issues.

The court cards can mean a person or demeanour:

- Princess: The joy of life, passion and sexual attraction. Arrogance and egotism.

- Prince: Adventure, creativity and moving forward. Unrest and impatience.

- Queen: Transformation, maturity and independence. Jealousy.

- Knight: The broadening of horizons, humanitarianism. Restriction, the prevention of growth.

Cups

Cups represent the element of Water, the emotions. Are you a still pond with all sorts of things going on underneath or are you a raging sea making yourself heard? This is the suit associated with all forms of love.

- Ace: New love, longing for affection, harmony. Vagueness and panic.

- Two: Perfect union, the highest form of love, happiness. Conflict and separation.

- Three: Conception, inner growth, fulfilment in love. Lust, sexual promiscuity.

- Four: Caring, nurturing, motherhood love. Emotional possessiveness.

- Five: Disappointment and pain, separation and bitterness. Great change.

- Six: Pleasure, a sexual encounter, charisma. Detachment from reality.

  Seven: Intoxication, escapism through indulgence. Addiction and lies.

- Eight: Resignation to your fate, seclusion. Depression, self-pity.

- Nine: Happiness, the chance to make a wish, redemption. Vanity and arrogance.

- Ten: Completion and fulfilment, optimism. A feeling of emptiness.

The court cards can mean a person or demeanour:

- Princess: Exploring your inner emotions, intuition. Love as a weapon.

- Prince: Devotion, love, sympathy, warmth. Naïvety, selfishness.

- Queen: Inner wisdom, seeing beyond the veil. Vagueness and irrational fears.

- Knight: A healer, an emotional man, intuition. Instability, helping others but not yourself.

Swords

Here we have the element of Air, the rush of wind that brings communication and clear direction. Are you the sort who just wafts along or will you be travelling like a force-ten gale? Thoughts and the mind are this suit's domain.

- Ace: A new idea, objectivity, solutions not problems. Being weak-willed and restless.

- Two: The need for balance, diplomacy and ears, not mouths. Unresolved issues.

- Three: Sorrow, grief and tears from feeling helpless. Purpose, wholeness.

- Four: Keeping still, a truce, justice and tolerance. An illness to force rest.

- Five: Seeing your limits, venting anger appropriately. Harm, a turn for the worse.

- Six: A search for the truth (it's the search that's important). Mistrust, scepticism.

- Seven: Shrewdness. Intrigue and craftiness, misguided trust.

- Eight: Interference, nervousness and gossip. A sharp tongue.

- Nine: Cruelty. This is my second card that says, 'Stop reading.' Overcoming fear.

- Ten: Ruin, departure, the final word. A necessary abandonment which will be for the good.

The court cards can mean a person or demeanour:

- Princess: Hastiness, dispassion, objectivity. Aggressiveness and rebelliousness.

- Prince: Erratic change, overcoming obstacles through will. Clumsiness and curtness.

- Queen: Self-determination, freedom and independence. Being too cool and distant.

- Knight: Astuteness, keenness and intelligence. Too much thought and not enough emotion.

Disks

Here we have Earth as the element. This is related to the slow, dependable and reliable march of the seasons – sow, reap, sow, reap. Are you ready to grow or have things got to the point where cutting back is the only option? Disks also represent money and health.

- Ace: Great happiness and contentment, a great idea. Financial arrogance.

- Two: Change within two weeks or two months. Instability and flexibility.

- Three: Hard work brings results slowly but surely. Lack of direction.

- Four: Security and power, a fortress. Stubbornness and stagnation.

- Five: Worry, crisis, upheaval and forced change. Failure, a test!

- Six: Success and abundance, overcoming obstacles, prosperity. Life out of balance.

- Seven: Failure and disintegration, emptiness. Confrontation and blockages.

- Eight: Taking a step back and getting perspective, self-discipline. Lack of order.

- Nine: Joy and gain, especially financial. Good money sense. Empty pockets!

- Ten: Wealth and power given after hard work. Greed and dictatorship.

The court cards can mean a person or demeanour:

- Princess: Security, love and warmth. Over-sentimentality.

- Prince: Physical exercise and wellbeing. Stubbornness and lack of movement.

- Queen: Opulence, a stable family, fertility. Looking in the wrong direction.

- Knight: Striving for security, a healer, endurance. Over-cautiousness, jealousy.

Laying Out the Cards

There are many different ways to lay out the cards. You will no doubt find them all in time, but to begin with it's best to concentrate on two basic systems, which I'll outline here. One is the three-card lay and the other is the classic Celtic Cross.

Remember, you can ask any question you want; just be clear about your intention and aware that the Tarot will suggest an outcome rather than give a 'yes' or 'no' answer.

Bearing in mind that presently you are concentrating on developing your skills, you might want to base your question around that. Questions such as 'How will my skills develop?' or perhaps 'What needs to change in my life in order for my subconscious to open up?' might be useful. You decide, it's your lay. If you're doing this with friends, decide on a common question. That just makes the analysis simpler.

The Three-Card Spread

This very simple spread is the one I use most. It helps me make decisions, it colours my life with suggestions and information that I might otherwise have missed and, to be honest, it often confirms what I have been thinking all along!

Ask your question and select your cards, then place them in front of you like this:

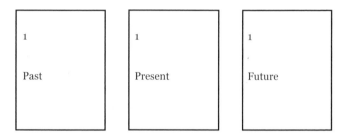

Easy peasy. Now interpret your cards! To help you, here's an example.

Question: How will my spiritual development go?

Interpretation

In the past you may have been full of good ideas but never really taken action simply because you never felt driven enough, but recently a teacher, either earthly or otherwise, may have entered your life to help you take your psychic development further. Creativity and your ability to get excited about the future and the possibilities it holds will take you on to brighter things.

◆ ◆ ◆ ◆

That's it. It needn't be an essay. Take what you can from the cards and don't force things – padding everything out with psychic-babble is not required!

If you want, you can put another card on top of an original card for clarity. That's absolutely fine, but if you find yourself taking another and another, you might as well go for another lay and ask another question. Knowing when to stop is the sign of a good reader. You will know it when you find yourself thinking it!

Look out also for the same cards making an appearance time and time again. When they do that, lift the repeating card out and put another three underneath for clarification.

Don't be afraid to get creative. I know I have said that over and over, but I make no apologies for it!

The Celtic Cross

This lay is a little more complex and, to be honest, it takes some getting used to, but it's worth the effort.

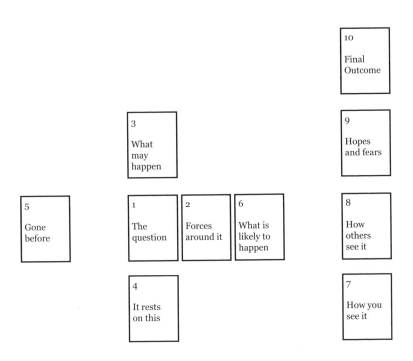

As ever, here's an example!

Question: How will my psychic development affect my life?

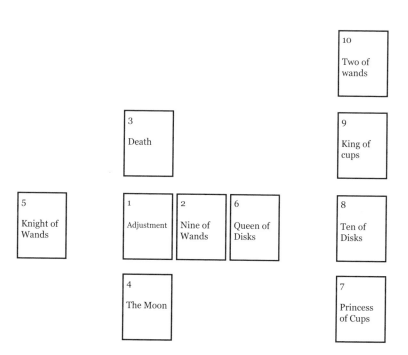

Interpretation

Adjustments will have to be made for you to fulfil your destiny and although you are fully aware of the preparations you have to make, there may be more sacrifices than you are initially aware of. Transformation will come from being more in touch with your subconscious and the knowledge you have gathered up until now. You should be prepared to look at lessons learned and to remember your longing for union with the divine. Others will support you in your search, perhaps even financially, and although you may fear instability, you can hope for intuitive and willing forces and are likely to get them. Ultimately, you will be in control and have the creativity you need to succeed.

What's interesting for me is I didn't orchestrate these cards, I simply sat and asked my own cards to show me how the reader of this book might experience their development.

I could go over that interpretation now and pick out the keywords for each card and just how I got there, but I'm not – you are. The way I saw it is on page 204. Remember it's not about being right or wrong, it's simply about being!

Consolidation

The only thing you can do with the Tarot is practise, practise, practise. Look at at least one card a day. Take it in the morning with your multi-vitamin! Ask for a card to help you with that day's events, see where it goes and learn as you live your life – how marvellous.

The meditation exercise you did earlier is great and simply losing yourself in the cards can really help, but there's nothing like using them to make it all happen.

◆ ◆ ◆

Later on we will be coming back to the Tarot and tying it in with numerology. This will give you another layer of information, so that's something to get excited about!

There are many other cards you can use, angel cards and fairy cards being among the most popular. These work on the same principle of sending a message in picture form to your subconscious, and they work very well! Experiment with them, trust your intuition and if you feel drawn to them, stop dithering about, get a pack and see what they have to say to you!

CHAPTER 8

NUMEROLOGY

As my own training took on a deeper meaning I began questioning things more and more and I also began to see things that would have otherwise escaped my notice. One thing I noticed with the Tarot was that certain numbers came up all the time. I had a run of threes, then a spate of fives... I recognized that the groups of numbers must have some relevance to numerology, so that seemed like a natural place for me to look next.

As with astrology and Tarot, numerology links to all that I have been taught. There are 12 houses in astrology, 10 planets, 12 signs; in Tarot each card bears a number, be it Major or Minor Arcana. Pretty soon I was finding numbers everywhere and then I found myself unpeeling another layer in the game of understanding my psychic self. It's a bit like 'Cosmic Sesame Street' – your life brought to you by the number 3!

Now I can feel you already worrying about all those logarithms and calculus problems that may be coming your way, but there's no need! The hardest thing you will have to do here is add up, and even then you can use a calculator if you're feeling lazy. I still use one now and again – just to make sure I have it right, of course!

Numbers are hailed by some as the building blocks of the universe. Where they come from is shrouded in mystery, but

Pythagoras might have had a theory on that one. Numbers are all around us, but using them properly means having a purpose in using them. I want to use them to show you even more aspects of your psychic self, to give you as much information on your cosmic blueprint as possible. The more information you have, the more you can let go and trust your intuition to show you the way forward.

As with most of the disciplines in this book, the study of numerology goes on forever, but this will get you started, putting that first foot out. All you need to have to hand is your birth date and your birth name. OK? Not exactly brain-crunching so far!

📖   Stop for a moment and ask yourself what your favourite number is. Write it down in your journal.

It will be interesting to see just what that intuitive thought alone can tell you about yourself and whether or not that number comes up for you later when we look at your four core numbers. Your what?

Your Four Core Numbers

There are lots of ways to use numbers, but four core numbers will bring you a lot of information about yourself and you will be pleasantly surprised at just how much they resonate with you. They are:

- your life path number

- your destiny number

- your soul number

- your personality number.

Think of them as a combination that will open up the safe that holds your cosmic blueprint. You can find out what they are from your birth date and your birth name. More on that later.

For now, just to start you off, let's do a really simple exercise.

Think about your birthday – just the day, not the year. What number is it? Think of yourself as that number. I was born on 8 June, for example, so that makes me an 8. In numerology you reduce every number to a single digit, so if you were born on the 23rd of the month, 2 + 3 = 5, so you will be a 5. Easy peasy.

If your birthday number reduces to 11 or 22, very significant numbers, still reduce them to single digits, but write them like this: 11/2 or 22/4. The numbers 11, 22, 33, 44, etc., are called master numbers. More about them later, it's just important you know this from the start.

Here's what your number reveals about you:

1. You are an independent person, a leader, someone who wants to be seen at the front of the pack, someone who creates new paths rather than follows well-worn routes.

2. You are a good team player and best when in a part-

nership. Diplomatic, you want to be seen as the balancer. You love to be surrounded by beauty and luxury.

3. Childlike joy shines through in your approach to people. You love to be creative and flit from party to party.

4. Hard-working and practical, you are concerned with putting down strong foundations and being seen as self-disciplined and fair-minded.

5. You love change for change's sake and don't do patience! (*Note to other numbers*: When you meet a 5, beware! You could fall in lust all too quickly!)

6. Artistic and full of idealistic plans, you want a soft velvet world where chocolate is free! Family and other animals are favoured, and not surprisingly so is romance.

7. What does all this mean? Whatever it is, you are likely to find out by locking yourself away and thinking it through. A private number.

8. You want to be the boss! Even in relationships, you are highly competent and full of confidence, especially when handling big projects.

9. Broad-minded, you will put up with most people and appreciate them for their differences. You want to make the world a better place to live in.

Was that fun? I bet now you're looking at the numbers for your family and friends as well, and if you've just met someone you're thinking either 'Cancel that date' or 'Bring it forward!' Just come back to yourself for now. You've time for all that sort of stuff later on. This is all about you. Let's look at your own special numbers.

Your Life Path Number

You can find out what your life path number is by reducing the numbers of your date of birth down to a single digit.

There are different theories on just how you do this. Do you add across, reduce as you go, add downwards or add any double digits together? For the purposes of this book, we will reduce first. Here's an example.

Say your date of birth is **18 October 1975**. That comes out as **18 + 10 + 1975**.

Reduce it first and you get 9 + 1 + 22 = 32. This then reduces to **5**.

♦♦♦♦

Mine is this: **8 June 1960**
    8 + 6 (sixth month of the year) + 7 (1+9+6+0) = 21 = 2 + 1 = 3

This gives me a life path number of **3**.

Write your life path number down. Remember if the numbers come out as **11, 22** or **33**, these are master numbers. Write them as **11/2, 22/4** and **33/6**. You will have to interpret both parts of these numbers.

We'll be looking more closely at the meaning of the numbers later. For now it's just about getting that overall blueprint. To help you, here are some keywords for the numbers. Remember, keywords are about helping you to kickstart your intuition and are by no means exhaustive.

Number	Keywords
1	Fresh start, leader; creative, innovative
2	Balance, relationships; co-operative
3	Truth, optimism; playful, expressive
4	Hard work, foundations; practical
5	Change, freedom; successful, resourceful
6	Family, service to others; dutiful, hardworking
7	Science, solitude; spiritual, mystical
8	Power, business; financially astute, self-assured
9	Conclusion, teaching; knowledgeable, transformative
Master	Numbers
11	Teacher of truth; uplifting
22	Master builder, architect of a better world; inspiring
33	Master of compassion, teacher; creative

As you can see, the master numbers indicate a higher calling, as you might have suspected. Later we'll take a closer look, but now it's time to discover your destiny number.

Your Destiny Number

I want to add something else to the mix – letters as numbers. This is essential for turning your name, address, dog's name, in fact any name you like, into a number.

First here's what's assigned where:

1	2	3	4	5	6	7	8	9
A	B	C	D	E	F	G	H	I
J	K	L	M	N	O	P	Q	R
S	T	U	V	W	X	Y	Z	

It's fairly obvious how they run – you simply assign A to 1, B to 2, etc. – and if you want to convert someone's name into numbers it's easy enough to draw your own table. In fact, why don't you do it right now? That way you will be on your way to remembering it even more!

Now take the letters of your name and match up the numbers. Here's mine as an example:

D	4	W	5
A	1	E	5
V	4	L	3
I	9	L	3
D	4	S	1

Total: **22** (for 'David') and **17** (for 'Wells')
= **4** + **8** = **12** = **3**

My destiny number is **3**.

A word on names

Before you have a go, just a quick word on names. Make sure the name you use for numerology is the one on your birth certificate. Shortened names like Nick instead of Nicholas or Jen instead of Jennifer aren't allowed, so stop right there and use your full name, Engelbert Humperdinck. If you have more than one middle name, like my mum, who has four, you do have to use them all, I'm afraid.

What if your name has changed? Use your original one. However, if you were adopted and your name was changed but you know your original name, go with the name you know. By all means look at the original one as well, if you like, but this may show you more about where you have come from rather than who you are now. You could see your original name as your given path and your adopted one as what you have chosen!

Similarly, if you are a married woman who has changed her surname, use your maiden name for the purposes of numerology. Your married surname is another energy you can add to your numerology profile as a lesson you have taken on. It's not, however, part of your original cosmic blueprint.

◆ ◆ ◆ ◆

Now that's sorted, why not have a go at working out your destiny number? What does it come out as? Write it down! What next?

Your Personality Number

Now your personality number. That's arrived at by adding the numerical value of the consonants in your name, for example:

D	4	**W**	5
A		E	
V	4	**L**	3
I		**L**	3
D	4	**S**	1

This gives us **12 + 12 = 3 + 3 = 6**

My personality number is 6.

What's yours? Write it down with the other two.

Your Soul Number

Only one more to go, and it's your soul number. This is achieved by adding up the vowels in your name.

Once more using mine:

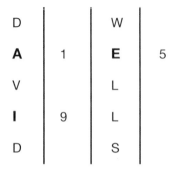

D		W	
A	1	**E**	5
V		L	
I	9	L	
D		S	

So, it's **10 + 5 = 1 + 5 = 6**

My soul number is **6**.

Now it's your turn. Get the last part of your code together, then that's all the maths done for now!

Summary

Here's a quick review of how you find those four numbers:

Number	Formula
Life path number	Your birth date numbers
Destiny number	The letters of your full birth name
Personality number	The consonants of your full birth name
Soul number	The vowels of your full birth name

Your Numerological Blueprint

Now write them out like this:

Life path number	3
Destiny number	3
Personality number	6
Soul number	6

That's my blueprint: 3 3 6 6. Write yours down. Why not make it your PIN number for your credit cards? That way your number will be getting an outing every time you use your card. Oops, have to change mine now!

So just how does that help you unlock your psychic self? Knowing how you resonate, how you vibrate if you like, means you can apply yourself to the task in hand in your own particular way. As you do so, you will find that things open up for you, simply because you are on the right path rather than trying to fight against the world to go heaven knows where. Knowing your blueprint will help you to truly focus not only on what you are good at but on what you came here to do!

Before we go any further, it's time to look at those master numbers in a little closer detail, just in case you came up with them in your blueprint.

Master Numbers

Master numbers indicate spiritual gifts that go beyond the norm. They don't automatically say you are psychically gifted, that's a different thing altogether, but they say the potential is there. You are the one who must unlock it. The way to do this can often come through a series of tests and trials that can make learning a challenge. It's not always a bed of roses. The difference is ego. There's no room for it with master numbers, certainly not the ego that thinks it's better than anyone else, anyway. There's nothing wrong with confidence – that's entirely different!

All master numbers from 11 to 99 share some common ground, traits that are recognizable to all who have eyes to see. Master number types have a need to be master of their own destiny. People seem drawn to them for information, normally of a spiritual nature. Sometimes they seek fame in order to pass their message on to a greater audience. They definitely never think small – it's big, big, big. They usually require time on their own to recharge their batteries, which can be depleted very easily, especially when they have an emotional moment, which they can do all too frequently. They are on a mission to serve and to raise the vibration of humanity.

Although master numbers do go all the way up from 44 to 99, these are rare, which is why we will look at 11/2, 22/4 and 33/6 for the purposes of this adventure.

11/2. Bright, inspiring, full of nervous energy, you seek spiritual truth and bring that to others. You can be a visionary who loves to be centre stage, especially if talking about spiritual matters. I liken this master number to Mercury, messenger of the gods. Light of foot, you are the go-between of Heaven and Earth.

22/4. A master of organization, you like major projects to get stuck into. Idealistic and a natural leader, you can be highly disciplined but are also intuitive and not afraid to use that in a world where intuition may not be as prized as it should be. Honest and highly able, you are ready to work for what you believe in.

33/6. Highly sensitive, caring and mystical, you make sacrifices for others. You are sympathetic, big-hearted and emotional, a champion of the underdog, and will take on the worries of others perhaps a little too easily. You bring healing through compassionate understanding.

Now let's look at all your four core numbers in closer detail, beginning with your life path number.

Your Life Path Number

- Comes from your birth date.

- Illuminates your path.

- Indicates talents.

You can change your name, where you live and even your favourite number, but you can't change your birth date, which is probably why your life's path is dictated by it. It's similar to your birth chart in a way, which is hardly surprising, as they both use the same piece of information as a starting-point.

This number gives you an idea of what you are likely to find satisfying in life. It can show you the truth of those burning desires for change!

Life Path Numbers

1. Independence is the key for you. You must travel the road you choose and usually you must be right out in front of everyone else! This will teach you how to be what you must be: a leader. Great places for you to work are those which allow you to go off and break new ground. If you have to follow anyone else, it just makes things difficult!

2. You must have another person alongside you. Company along the way is what counts! You are one of life's counsellors, but that means you must first learn how to relate to another person. Early on one-on-ones may not be easy, but once you get the hang of dealing with another person, you can use those skills to your advantage. You make a great mediator and, of course, counsellor.

3. Spontaneity is important for you. Without it you stagnate and nobody wants that! Bringing joy and happiness into your life means shifting and changing more quickly than a shifting and changing thing, so get on with it! Communication is what you're all about – without mobiles and e-mail on the go, just what would you do? You would sit in coffee shops gossiping, that's what. Writing, speaking and dancing are good for you – not all at once, though!

4. Managing everyone's affairs means you have to learn what happens when things are thrown into chaos, and you will early on. That done, you can get on with building better structures and showing those around you how to do the same. A great eye for detail makes you a fantastic accountant as well as jewel thief. Only you could figure a way through that alarm system!

5. Sales and marketing, bigging it up and talking it down, that's what you're all about. You're not someone who hears the same beat as the rest of us, which is fine as long as you remember to use that rather than try to fit in. You were made to stand out, to be the one everyone notices when you enter a room. Travel, trendy places and advertising agencies suit you well.

6. People are likely to search for you in their time of need and so medicine is a world you may fit into very well. Therapy where you can give that special one-on-one care and see the results of your efforts works well too. That means everything from beauty therapy to rehabilitation!

7. An analytical person, you will want to test everything and record the results in a methodical way. That makes you a keen scientist as well as a technology-lover. Oddly, this number also resonates with people looking for higher spiritual knowledge. Combining the two can work very well. You make a great technician and could gravitate towards teaching in whichever field you choose to work in.

8. Born to be the boss, you don't do well at being told what to do. You want to be the one doing the telling, which is fine when you're at work, not so great in relation-ships! People naturally come to you for help and might even expect you to make some decisions for them – do so if you wish, but remember the karma that might be involved in that one! Wherever you choose to work you will be top of your profession.

9. Universal love sounds wishy-washy to some, but for you it simply means being able to see the way ahead more clearly than most. A natural healer and able to take that to people through the arts, you understand the need for beauty in the world. Humanitarian issues will fire you up and get you involved.

11/2. A born leader, you are ready to shine your light for others to follow, and follow they will. You will end up in a position of authority where others will want to listen to what you have to say. Be prepared to stand up and be counted.

22/4. Having a vision and then being able to make that vision manifest is your task. You are a person of your word – if you say something will happen, it will happen – and building better structures is your goal, be they actual buildings or simply better ways of living.

33/6. You just can't help yourself, can you? There you are, offering people a glimpse of what it would be like to simply be happy with what you're doing and where you're doing it! You shine through your example to others and teach as a consequence.

This is just a taster. It goes on forever. There's more to learn than we have space for, but that's the exciting thing. Once you have the basics you will want to explore more – and the more you explore, the more you will want to explore!

Your Destiny Number

- Comes from adding the numerical values of the letters in your full name.

- Shows your purpose.

- Sets the benchmark.

When you know where you're heading, it's easier to get there. A lot of your spiritual development is based on just that. Your destiny number can help you to see where it is you're going.

As well as your full name, think about your first name, any middle names and your last name as lessons on their own, aside from your four blueprint numbers. Your first name gives your personal destiny, your middle name can show you things you may not necessarily like and may choose to keep hidden, and your last name obviously tells you the traits you have inherited from your family.

Destiny Numbers

1. Your mission in life, and you cannot really choose to ignore it, Special Agent No. 1, is to make sure you become the leader of the team. Take control of those who need your help and lead the way by showing the way. New, new, new you are and example is your greatest gift. Set a good one and watch people flock to follow.

2. A diplomat's life is not an easy one, but it's rewarding when two sides who may not have sat down at the table together before your arrival finally get around to talking. You're not only a team player, you're a team maker. Happily, you are not destined to do this alone and being part of a strong partnership of your own will help your cause immensely.

3. Inspire me. Go on, say something inspiring – you know you can! Make me feel like getting up and doing things I never thought I could, and then inspire me to do some more. That's your destiny and you can do it not only with a smile on your face but by putting one on mine with your wit and charm!

4. Put that shoulder to the grindstone and get on with some hard work. Thanks! It's not all bad news – you are good at what you do, no, great at what you do, and the reward will be security, something you value highly. Traditional family values are important to you and even if sometimes you feel like digging in and being stubborn, you will get up and get on with things all over again tomorrow.

5. As the changeling, you are called upon to be fluid and flexible, to be ready to do whatever it takes to make something work and all the time to do it with the freedom of your own creativity. Sometimes you will be restless and that could lead you to being fed up. The solution is change – change something today and tomorrow will be different.

6. Get yourself an apron and be ready to serve. Oh, all right, it's not that bad, but you will want to nurture your family and friends and to make your world and theirs a better place to be. As long as you don't make a martyr out of yourself they will respect your help rather than take advantage of your gifts. Try to maintain a balance between giving and receiving to get the most out of your number.

7. Seek and record your findings. The trainspotter of the numerological world you may be, but digging into the detail of things brings you knowledge and by observing closely you see what other people inevitably miss. Occasionally your anorak might get in a tangle when those you love don't appreciate all your efforts, but more often than not you will be the one with the solution to their worries.

8. Total control over yourself sounds a little too clinical – maybe it's better to say you are on a path that puts you in charge. Extending your unrivalled organizational skills to the world at large makes you a contender in the business world and success is assured, even if now and again you're a little too over the top for some! Possessions, lots of them and well earned, are yours.

9. Reach out and touch somebody's hand, make this world a better place if you can – Diana Ross could have sung those lyrics for you. Perfect unconditional love isn't something you see every day. It may be a challenge, but it's one that's within your grasp. Sometimes you just won't feel that fluffy. That's fine, as long as you remember it's a sign to hitch up your wagon and go broaden your horizons.

11/2. Inspire others, make those around you want to run around singing out how joyous they feel! You are likely to be put in a position where you can reach a lot of people with your message of hope and joy. Lead them towards bigger and better things by showing them what can happen when you embrace the fullness of life.

22/4. Build that hospital, open that school, raise the funds you need to make someone else's life better. That's your goal and you can score every time. Being practical and resourceful, you are able to get the help of others. Sometimes you may not want to get out of bed, but once you're there, you're there!

33/6. Without being too happy-clappy, your task is to show there's joy in embracing your spiritual side. What am I saying? You be as happy-clappy as you want, Number 33/6, it's what you do best! Sometimes it won't be easy, as you see what's wrong with the world all too clearly. Maybe that's the very thing that inspires you to inspire us?

Your Personality Number

- Comes from adding the numerical values of the consonants in your full birth name.

- Shows what you present to the world.

- Reveals the mask you wear.

Here's the outer you. In astrology this number is akin to the ascendant or rising sign, the part of your chart that tells people what to expect when they first meet you. It's your outer defence in many circumstances, but it's also what gets you noticed. It's the bit people are either attracted to or want to run away from, depending on whether you are wearing a tiara or throwing a tantrum.

Personality Numbers

1. You can appear a little overbearing, which is probably due to wanting to take charge of the situation, even if it is only the queue for a hamburger! Your creativity can often be expressed in what you wear, or are you just trying to stand out from the crowd?

2. Better at being approached than making the first move, you can come across as shy, but that's probably more about weighing others up than staying away from them. Once people get to know you they will see you're charming and a great listener and always willing to help others.

3. Buy a red nose and one of those tiny little cars where the doors fall off, and join a circus. Failing that, why don't you just keep us all entertained with your uplifting sense of humour and your charm – oh, you have them! Just remember the times when you need to be serious.

4. Frivolous nonsense doesn't do it for you; you prefer the practical things in life, even the cheaper things in life, but what's wrong with saving a penny or two? You are dependable and hardworking, that's a given, but try to make room for some spontaneity and letting go.

5. 'Attractive' is an odd concept. Surely that's a matter of who's doing the looking? But there are likely to be lots of people looking at you and I'm sure you'll take advantage of that. People are naturally drawn to you, which makes you a great salesperson. Travel and adventure feed you. Eat and drink of them often.

6. A natural-born teacher, you are able to help those

who can benefit from your experience and do it in such a way that they feel comfortable. You are good at solving dilemmas and helping others to see what they can do to make things better for themselves. In love you might want to separate fantasy from reality.

7. You probably don't want anyone getting too close too soon, which is why that look of disdain crosses your face so often – or is that your natural look? You like privacy and as a consequence can come across as aloof, but once people get to know you they recognize that's all about your own protection. Just try to come down from that ivory tower now and again.

8. The big shoulder pads of the 1980s must have been great for you, as power dressing is what you're all about! That doesn't only extend to your suit jackets – it seems that aura of control is what you do best, and to be fair it's because you *are* actually in control. Remember the top can be lonely, though. Allow some people to share it with you.

9. Waxing lyrical about the way other people should do this, that and the other is one thing, actually getting them to see that your wisdom can be practical may be another. Your challenge is to use your warmth and caring nature to show them rather than tell them – example over instruction.

11/2. With the 'X' factor shining out of every pore, it's not hard to see you in a crowd, but what can you do with all that glitter? You can show others how to use their own psychic ability in the way you intuitively use yours – to run your life. Just don't let the negativity of others slow you down.

22/4. Are you really as capable as you appear? I think you might be and those who know you would agree, most of the time. All you have to do is make sure you see enough of them to keep them reminded of that fact. Don't spend so much time at work that you lose the sense of what's really important.

33/6. Some may see you as having a little too much to say when they really don't think you should be saying anything at all. That would be because what you are saying is right, and frankly they don't like it. Carry on with your torch of truth – show them the way!

Your Soul Number

- Comes from adding the numerical values of the vowels in your full name.

- Suggests desires and the way to contentment.

- Shows what you need to feed your soul.

If your soul had a voice this number tells you what it would be saying. It shows what it wants, really, really wants. By now you ought to have a better idea yourself of what it is your soul desires, but use your soul number to check you're on the right path. To be honest, it's also good to make sure that your inner vibration matches your outer knowledge now and again! Remember your soul is the part of you that knows the plan more than most. It has inside information that can help you towards fulfilment by doing what it is you set out to do from the moment you incarnated.

This number helps in other ways too. Imagine knowing the soul number of your partner or your children. That would give you a greater understanding of where they were coming from and you would be able to understand, adapt to and help them much more quickly.

Soul Numbers

1. As you have learned by now, number 1 wants to be in the lead. You don't like being told what to do and are sometimes a little pushy, preferring to run the show than be part of the cast. In relationships with others you need to have a peer, someone who is as capable as you are. You don't really do weak and helpless.

2. Peace, love and understanding are what you give and what you need. You are great at calming things down, a real walking, talking United Nations, and as long as you know you are appreciated you will stick around. You work best when someone is beside you.

3. If you can make people laugh, you can have anything you want! You know how to get people motivated and although you yourself can run out of steam now and again, you can always find it in you to be the life and *soul* of the party. Sorry about that sad pun.

4. If anyone gets a pair of comfy slippers for Christmas, it's likely to be you who sent them! Practical rather than frivolous, you see the need to be prepared and to have a plan. In fact, if you don't have a plan, you plan to have a plan! You are an unparalleled organizer and we all need organization!

5. Don't fence me in! You need to know you can roam wherever and whenever you want, free from those who will try and rein you back in. Change is what you want and if it seems to be scarce, you can create a little bit of mischief to get it. For you, variety is the spice of life.

6. A real stay-at-home, you are best when surrounded by family and loyal friends. You appreciate loyalty and in return you are devoted to those you love. You are highly committed both in love and in your working life. Yours is not a number to be played with when it comes to affairs of the heart.

7. Cool, calm and collected, you can appear frosty and worse, but your detachment is more about needing solitude in order to learn more about the spiritual worlds you seem to live in. With this psychic soul number, you recognize that growth comes from silence and contemplation.

8. Who's in charge? You are, that's who! You are a hard worker, and successful at that, but you find business easier to deal with than emotions. That doesn't mean to say you don't do emotions, just rarely. Let's say you're unlikely to make a big effort on Valentine's Day.

9. Everything is beautiful in its own way. Can you see that? Of course you can and you won't mind telling others about it if you get the chance. Sacrificing your own needs for others also suits you. Don't go overboard, though – that may be something that needs to be looked at!

11/2. You are an emotional roller-coaster of a soul who learns through those ups and downs and then passes that knowledge on so others can grow more quickly. With this psychic number, you will often know what's right, but sometimes it's what's right for others rather than for your-self.

22/4. You need to touch what you have achieved, and what better way than bringing about reforms that will lead to better structures for those in need. Think hospital wards and schools here. If not creating actual buildings, you want to see people moving towards higher spiritual values. If only we were all like you!

33/6. You will give, give and give some more, regardless of what's being asked. You have incarnated to offer us all the chance to see that the answer to all our questions is a simple one: *love*.

Consolidation

There's so much more to do with your numbers, but for now it's time to look at what you have learned to date. As usual I can't tell you everything in such a short time, and to be fair you need time to assimilate what you have learned.

In your journal write down your numerological blue-print again; for example:

Life path number	3
Destiny number	3
Personality number	6
Soul number	6

Now remind yourself what each number represents.

Write a little piece on your life's journey based on that information. Here's mine to help you:

> *My life path is one governed by the number 3, the number of communication and self-expression, of bringing joy to those I talk to and inspiring them to be more creative in their life. My destiny (3) is to teach with the same expression of joy and to help those who seek it through words and the celebration of life. My 6 personality accepts the responsibility and although I might sometimes take things a little too seriously, I will always do what's expected of me. My soul (6) wants me to do my duty in a nurturing way without being so busy that people feel they can't approach me.*

This is only a brief example and yours can be as long as you want it to be. Really let go here, as this is another chance to contact your inner being, your psychic self. Let them talk to you, let them give you the words. The more you let everything just flow, the more you know you are communicating with the person you really are.

CHAPTER 9

MIX IT ALL UP!

There's a great correlation between all the subjects in this book. Tarot cards hold the astrological symbols in them, numerology can guide you to the Tarot and the chakras resonate with the lot! Add colour to your experiences by looking for links. Discovering them yourself will give you a greater understanding of the whole.

To help you on your way, here are some things for your journal, things you might want to look at. Apply them to day-to-day challenges or perhaps use them as a way to inspire yourself when you don't feel that great. I sometimes meditate using the Sun card, for example. It brightens me up and makes me realize that it's me that makes the difference to my day and not anyone else putting their stuff on my shoulders – even if it's the tax man demanding money!

Relationships are often a source of angst in life – certainly have been in mine. No matter how much I haven't wanted to see some of the things these tools were showing me, I have never doubted their wisdom. I remember a time when things weren't going that well with a partner and time after time both the Tarot and astrology were telling me it was the end of a cycle and time to realize it, but as we do I procrastinated. Finally I pulled myself together and trusted in my intuition and all the support these tools were giving me, and not only did I do the deed but within two weeks everything in my life turned for the better. It's amazing how one thing can block all the good that's out there for us to have.

Tarot Numbers

As an example of how the Tarot can link to numerology, take a look at the suits. They clearly all have numbers, one (ace) to ten. If one of these numbers is coming up a lot in your reading, then maybe it is telling you something, so look at the qualities of that number in your numerology profile and see what it is! The same goes in reverse. My core numbers, as you know, are 3 3 6 6, and the threes and sixes of the Tarot often come up in my own readings.

Here's a reminder of the meaning of the Tarot card numbers:

1. New beginnings, a fresh start, leadership, action.

2. Balance, union, diplomacy, marriage and the ability to hold energy.

3. Growth, creativity and the gift of making things happen, often through hard work.

4. Dependability, solidity (four sides to a square, four legs on a chair) and the family (astrologically, the fourth house in a chart rules the family).

5. The midpoint and therefore the turning point, but which way will it go?

6. Bringing things back into balance, doing what's needed after an upset.

7. A spiritual number that holds victory for those who make the effort.

8. Power and material gain, success in whatever you have worked at.

9. Not quite the end of the cycle, but almost. Wisdom through adversity.

10. The completion of a cycle and beginning of another. Can also mean overdoing things.

📖　Look at your life path number. What Major Arcana number is it? Mine is 3, which translates as the Empress.

Do the same with all your blueprint numbers. If your number comes out as a double digit under 21, read the double digit and then the reduced one for a greater understanding. For example, say you end up with 18, reduce it to 9, but with the Tarot read 18/9. This will give you the Moon and the Hermit. If this is your life path number, what does that mean? What if it's your destiny number?

Use your intuition to find a way – by now you ought to be taking control and doing what you feel, guided by all you have learned and all those seen and unseen who want to help, but ultimately it's your call and your consequences!

Going through Changes

As you move along your path of psychic development, it is

inevitable that you will change and some people may not like the changes. They may feel as if they don't belong with the new you or they could simply be unsure of their own role in your new life.

When I was in the midst of all my training I can remember one of my friends simply saying, 'You've changed,' and when I asked him how, he couldn't say, just that I was different, calmer and more self-assured. Surely that was a good thing? Not according to him; he liked the slightly less predictable me and missed the company of someone as reckless as he was. Needless to say he carried on being reckless and I carried on taking back control of my life.

There will also be those who will doubt you, who will tell you you can't do this, that or the other because; let's face it, you never could.

All these people are feeling the winds of change in their face and whilst you're using it to fill your sails, they are sensing a storm coming.

So how do you manage these changes?

Conflict

When the chips are down the vinegar will follow and there will be some people who will go a bit sour. Some people won't like what's happening because they can see that the power is shifting from them back to you – where it belongs. Part of me wants to say, 'Tough on them,' but my grown-up side would say that by helping them to understand what you are going through you will gain support rather than a huffy, moody individual who doesn't want to play anymore.

So what do you do when you know that some of the choices you have to make will not be well received? You still make them, that's number one. You still go on with what you know is right, but you do so with firm empathy!

The core of who you are has been established by now. What you are doing from here on is strengthening your right arm to wield your sword to cut away anything you don't need and your left arm to receive the rewards that are yours. Deep? You think about it.

The fun and games are far from over, but you should now be questioning everything you see and hear, putting your own spin on it and then acting on what *you* want.

Angry Head

As a spiritual being you are not allowed to get angry. Really? No, you can do what you want, and that includes getting angry, as long as you remember those consequences we have talked about, but here's the truth about anger.

Getting angry with someone, that is to say shouting and having a big old Mary Anne over something, is not anger, it's usually frustration. Frustration over your lack of setting bottom lines, your lack of faith in them, your inability to see that someone else has to travel their own path etc. You have already seen the word 'you' jump out at you, so there's no need for me to do this, but I will: YOU, YOU, YOU, YOU! That's what that's all about.

True anger should be something that motivates you into action, doing something about a situation and not placing blame. Gandhi was angry, Mother Teresa no doubt had her moments and I'm sure that Christ lost His temper on more than one occasion, all in the name of motivation. I am not suggesting that you have such a karmic role to play; equally, I am not suggesting that you don't. What I am saying is that anger can be one of the greatest gifts if used wisely.

📖 Now I want you to think for some time about these questions. Write your responses in your journal and discuss them with a mate, but write them down first.

- Do you lose your temper quickly?

- Does other people's inability to listen bother you?

- Do you explain yourself properly?

- Have you ever achieved anything important by screaming and shouting?

- Have screaming and shouting ever lost you something precious in your life?

- Can you see peace in anger?

- What do you think the difference between cold and hot anger is?

- Which historical fighter for truth do you admire and why?

Hopefully you will recognize that anger is one of your greatest tools, something you should use, not be used by.

Peace, Love and Understanding

Peace

Why would you want to put yourself into an area of conflict or disharmony in the first place? There can be no harmony without conflict, that's why. Conflict alerts you to the need for a resolution – or should I say evolution?

In order to achieve that, of course, you have to move forward and you cannot do that without action. As we have already established, action is often the result of anger, but what about peace? Can things be achieved when you are in a calmer state? What is peace anyway? Floating around on a cloud of perfection with chubby-faced cherubs singing might sound like peace, but it would wear pretty thin very quickly if that was all it were. If you have fought hard to be where you are, aren't you stronger for it, more confident in what you know? Is that real peace?

You should now be seeing this state more and more in your life. It's a 'been there, seen that and got the T-shirt' place. It's a place of peace gained through recognizing the cycles of energy and what you can and can't do within them, and putting that into action – an active peace if you like!

Love

At the heart of all this is an acceptance of the higher forms of love – love for and from your soul, for your personality and for those around you. Love is one of those words that can sound a little too chocolate box to some, but believe me it is actually the answer to everything!

If you don't believe me, think about a situation at work, at home, wherever really, and follow this meditation.

Prepare in the normal way.

See in your mind's eye the situation you are having difficulty with. Perhaps someone at work is being far from pleasant or you are having relationship difficulties.

Now wrap that situation in pink light. Just flood it with that light until all you can see is the pink light.

Concentrate on it for a while and feel the light healing whatever the problem is.

Return your consciousness back to the room when you are ready.

Now watch the situation change!

The beauty of this visualization is that you can do it anywhere. How about just before an important meeting or a date that you want to go really well?

Often people find accepting love harder than giving it, which might sound a little odd, but ask yourself how you react when love is expressed to you. Do you feel worthy of it? Are you embarrassed if someone hugs you and says they love you? If you are, think about where that comes from. Is it something you learned in your formative years or perhaps in a past life?

You know by now how to find out, but why bother? Well, if you cannot receive love from others, how are you going to receive it from yourself?

There are classic signs that the personality and the soul are at odds with the love question, and here they are:

- You spend lots of money on things to cheer yourself up.

- You eat for comfort.

- You find relationships tough after a few months.

- Holding hands with you is like wrestling an alligator!

So what can you do about frosty knickers? I could say 'Open your heart' or something like 'Learn to love yourself' or maybe 'Release the love in you,' but mere words will not make the difference. What you need is understanding.

Understanding

Without this you cannot change anything, but I will be honest when I say that gaining it is one of the toughest challenges you will face. You have to climb a mountain here, but it will take you to one of the highest sources of love that you will ever touch. Are you ready?

📖 Prepare to meditate. Include the pillars.

Walk into your forest. Feel it, sense it all around you.

A path appears. Follow it. An animal moves ahead of you. What kind of animal is it?

Follow it until it takes you to the foot of a mountain, and watch as you see others coming down, smiling as they do so.

Now join the line of those waiting to climb the mountain and begin your journey.

Take your time. Follow in the footsteps of those who have gone before you.

With each step you feel lighter, more loved, closer to something so beautiful it almost hurts.

Snow appears as you get closer to the peak, making your journey harder, but still you go on.

As you round the peak you see a garden with a large house ahead of you. Go into it.

There are figures in robes standing in the garden and everyone seems to know which person to go to. Find your robed figure.

Stand in front of them and wait for them to hug you. How do you feel?

Release any emotion you feel now. Surround yourself with the universal love that they are offering you. Bask in your understanding of what it's like to be loved unconditionally.

They offer you a gift. Accept it graciously and note what it is.

Now say your goodbyes and prepare to come down the mountain. Do not be sad at your parting – this love surrounds you always.

Move slowly down the mountain, past those going up. As you pass them you cannot help but smile.

Now move back onto your own path, following your animal.

Let the animal fade and then the forest.

Bring your consciousness back into the room.

Time for tea and a chat – and a hug.

How do you feel? What was your animal? What was your gift? Who was your robed figure?

You have just met another guide. This guide will rarely

appear to you, but you will always know that they are there for you. Use the sensation of their energy when you are feeling disjointed in the world. Use it when you need a hug. Use it to remind yourself that you are loved.

Now that you have seen both sides of the path that deals with passion, which do you think you resonate with? Are you more likely to get things done with the fire of anger or the winds of peace? Do you overdo one side at the expense of the other or can you balance the two?

Remember that there is no right or wrong here. You are the one who makes the choices, you are the one who has the might and forgiveness at your disposal.

Silence Is Golden

But your eyes still see – in fact they see better when your mouth and ears are closed!

If you think about what you have learned so far, most of it has been very busy. There you've been, zipping around doing this, sorting that, standing up for yourself and even in your more peaceful times your head has been planning the next stage. Now is the time to stop and take stock, look around you and see, just see.

This point of observation is the refinement of your soul into that part of you which is spirit. In plain language that's the bit that knows neither fear nor celebration, neither right nor wrong, simply what is.

There is a starkness in this point that may become a bit too much on occasions, but let me tell you that sorrow is as much a part of your being as joy and love and as such it deserves your attention. If you have not felt sorrow, I doubt you would have got this far in your development. Without grief, you have learned nothing of love. If you are a parent, you will know the sorrow of letting your child grow into the world, watching it make its own way and not having to rely on you. That's joy and sorrow in one. In fact, parenthood is a great way of understanding this phase in your growth – standing by, waiting and watching, ready to step in if asked or needed.

Silence and watchfulness also have many uses. When you are caught between a rock and a hard place, for example, you have nowhere to go, so go nowhere. Stay where you are and watch as others give their story away via their actions.

📖   Today I want you to step outside an issue that is going on around you. If it is at work, tell your friends that you don't really want to go into it and to forget the latte and Danish pastry at eleven. If it's with a partner, smile sweetly and say that tonight you are having a 'me' night in, complete with facial, long hot bath and glass of Chardonnay – and no, they are not invited.

Listen to music, beautiful music, and relax a little, but above all remain as silent as you can. There can be noise around you, that is fine, but there should be as little from you as you can get away with.

Just do it for one day or night, whatever you can manage.

Now what did you learn? What illuminations came out of it? Who has shown themselves to be the instigator of all the chaos? What path has your clarity of vision shown you?

Let me share a story with you. A client of mine, we will call him Mark, came to me tired and emotional. More than anything, a feeling of fear surrounded him.

After preliminary chats about his life, hopes and ideals, it was clear that Mark was an extremely sensitive young man – sensitive in the true sense of the word, i.e. he picked up on others' moods without reservation and assumed that any discomfort was his. It's human nature (some humans anyway) to find people like Mark and latch onto them. Those who do this then drain the individual concerned and leave feeling much better, thank you very much. Remind you of anything?

Mark was no Buffy, but he did have a spark of determination in him that he and I were determined to turn into a raging fire.

Most of Mark's life had been spent in a quiet place. He had been a protected child, gone to a small school, then on to a fairly non-eventful university education. The problem started, as so many do, with his first relationship.

Mark was smitten and did all that he could for his girlfriend. She, on the other hand, was clearly not so committed and took all she could, then ran. Mark was devastated and it showed, but when you are the one who provides the answers for everyone else, where do you go? In his case nowhere.

By now Mark was on the other side of the lack of silence, not over-talking, but over-listening! There was a lot of work to do and we started in the normal way, with an analysis of his life, his dreams, wants and needs, and then looked at how he responded in different situations.

Mark was doing very well until it came to tackling the vampires that were surrounding him! He just couldn't imagine not helping his friends. He wouldn't have dreamed of stepping back and not getting emotionally involved with their problems – until he realized something.

One of Mark's friends had been going through a particularly difficult time and couldn't talk to his wife about a problem they were having, so in rode Mark on his white horse and acted as go-between. He resolved the situation, but at the cost of his own health and at the expense of a new relationship of his own. Then the cycle began again when the same friend found the same thing happening. Luckily, by now Mark was in a better place to understand what it was all about: the reason his friend was in the situation again was that he hadn't dealt with it first time round. Mark had.

This time, by stepping back and maintaining a silence on the matter, Mark helped his friend much more than he ever could have done by getting involved. More importantly, he helped *himself* by saving his energy!

It sounds very simple, but take a look at your own life and ask yourself where you are being drawn into things that are nothing to do with you. What does it do to you? And what could you do with all that extra energy?

Universal Grief

Often at this time in your development you can feel a little upset, a bit tearful and yet nothing is really that bad, so what's up?

The answer is that you can be picking up on world grief. Well, get you being such a spiritual being that you have the weight of the world on your shoulders!

It's no joke really, as I well know. This feeling often comes to me when I would least like it. So how do you deal with it? I would advise linking it with periods of grief that you are aware of, as the process involved in dealing with both is the same: *be still and enjoy it.*

Not as mad as it sounds. There are many ways of doing it – see what works for you. For me, it's choral music, blinds closed and tears until they cannot flow anymore – and you're right, that doesn't sound like much fun!

It isn't *meant* to be fun. What it is meant to do is to allow the channel to open between your spirit, soul and personality and back again to the universe that you are part of. It allows you to express your sorrow and not to bottle it up, which can result in resentment, moodiness and reaching for a crutch you don't need, like food or alcohol.

If you feel you carry too much grief all the time, that's a different story and I would urge you to contact a counsellor or professional organization that can help you further. The process described here is for clear events and single days when you feel that universal grief.

A Word to the Wise

Above the temple at Delphi are the words 'Know Thyself' and that is, after all, what you are attempting to do with psychic development – to understand who you are. Do you think you're there yet? Are you beginning to be wise?

'Wisdom' is a word that cannot be described in words. It's a feeling, a recognition from your peers, perhaps. It's an action. It cannot be learned from a book or from any kind of knowledge alone. You can be knowledgeable and still be a fool.

So how wise are you? Do you feel wise? What does wise feel like?

📖   Prepare to meditate. Include the four pillars.

Walk into your forest.

Now see whatever it is you see. That's right – no visuals from me. You are on your own.

Now write up your experience, discuss it and realize that from now on you can use your own spiritual power whenever you want. I'm so proud!

CHAPTER 10

LIFE AND HOW
TO GET ONE

During the course of your psychic development you will start to see things differently. You will be aware of the pitfalls and even when you do stumble into one - and yes, it will still happen - you will get out of it more quickly as well as know where to go next. When you feel 'No, I'm not going to go down that road again' or 'I have had enough, now it's time for a change,' you know you are in touch with your psychic self.

As I became more aware I noticed I was much more definite in my decision making, not to the point of foolishness or stubbornness, but in a more self-assured way. When that happens, it's usually a real show of just how far you have come.

You may still want to back up decisions with your new knowledge, and to be honest I still do that on an almost weekly basis, but the real joy lies in your ability to not only help yourself but also to help those around you. My golden rule on this one is never offer, always wait to be asked. If you are asked and feel it appropriate, then you can help. Help without being asked is called interference. One of my all-time annoying things is someone spontaneously coming up to you and starting on a reading, telling you how things are going to be! Now you know yourself how things are going to be, and what's more, it's you who's going to make them so.

I am often asked what tools I would use for what situation and I always answer by reminding people that the only rule is to have no rules! In getting to the point where you are reading this book I have carried around in my head for so long, I have used Tarot, astrology, numerology and good old-fashioned shutting up and listening to my inner and outer guides. When and how varied according to how I felt and what I felt was the most effective or obvious to use.

For short answers the Tarot is best for me. That's answers to questions like 'What happens if I choose this route or that one?' For a long-term view, say to judge my best strategy for career development, I use astrology.

Yearly Review

Have you ever wondered where the saying 'Many happy returns' comes from? It's a reference to astrology. A return is when a planet comes full circle to the point it was at when you were born and as the Sun takes one year to make that journey, it's this luminary that people are referring to on your birthday. Many happy returns is your solar return, the return of the Sun to the exact degree of your birth.

All very interesting, but how can it help you? Get in touch with your local friendly astrologer before your birthday and you will see. A solar return chart will give you a photograph of your year ahead. Couple it with your own Tarot spread for your year ahead, do the numerology for your birthday year and you will have a plan that's achievable because it's there waiting for you!

I always do this around May, bearing in mind I was born

in June. It gives me some idea of what's going on and as well as looking ahead, it helps me review the year just gone - a sort of psychic MOT. Make it your own, develop a system you can use year after year and be active in your future rather than passive.

◆ ◆ ◆ ◆

Eventually, all things psychic will be inbuilt and become as natural as breathing. As for me, not a day goes by when I don't think above the earthly day-to-day tasks and connect to the higher truths that surround us. When you begin to do the same - and you will - you will find that things that used to bother you are of no concern. You will see them for what they are and start to concentrate on what's important: your own development and through that your ability to help others.

Blessed Be.

RESOURCES

www.orderofthewhitelion.com
A great teaching site run by my own teacher.

◆◆◆◆

www.isisworkshops.co.uk
Friendly affordable workshops taught by two exceptional women.

◆◆◆◆

The Astrological Association of Great Britain
Unit 168
Lee Valley Technopark
Tottenham Hale
London N17 9LN
Tel: +44 (0)208 880 4848/fax 4849
www.astrologer.com/aanet
A great site for information on courses and finding local astrologers.

People often ask where I buy my crystals – here it is!
AristiA
233 Albert Road
Southsea
Portsmouth
PO4 0JR
Tel: +44 (0)23 92 355 645
www.aristia.co.uk

And the greatest resource of all: LIFE.

◆ ◆ ◆ ◆

Tarot interpretation
Adjustments (obvious one!) will have to be made for you to fulfil your destiny and although you are fully aware of the preparations (Nine of Wands) you have to make, there may be more sacrifices (Death) than you are initially aware of. Transformation (Death) will come from being more in touch with your subconscious (the Moon) and the knowledge (Knight of Wands) you have gathered up until now. You should be prepared to look at lessons learned (Queen of Disks) and to remember your longing for union with the divine (Princess of Cups). Others will support you in your search, perhaps even financially (Ten of Disks), and although you may fear instability, you can hope for intuitive and will-ing forces (King of Cups) and are likely to get them. Ultimately, you will be in control and have the creativity you need to succeed (Two of Wands).

FURTHER READING

Books

Spirit Messenger, by Gordon Smith

The Unbelievable Truth, by Gordon Smith

Through my Eyes, by Gordon Smith

Stories from the Other Side, by Gordon Smith

If You Could See What I See, by Sylvia Browne

Conversations with the Other Side, by Sylvia Browne

Spirit&Destiny Soul Secrets, edited by Emily Anderson

After Life, by John Edward

Crossing Over, by John Edward

Diary of a Psychic, by Sonia Choquette

Trust Your Vibes, by Sonia Choquette

The Complete Book of Numerology,
by David A. Phillips

Ask and It Is Given, by Esther and Jerry Hicks

The Amazing Power of Deliberate Intent,
by Esther and Jerry Hicks

Angel Therapy, by Doreen Virtue

Angel Visions, by Doreen Virtue

Daily Guidance from Your Angels, by Doreen Virtue

Goddesses & Angels, by Doreen Virtue

The Lightworker's Way, by Doreen Virtue

Messages from Your Angels, by Doreen Virtue

Card packs

5 Keys to Happiness Oracle Cards,
by Gordon Smith and Dronma

Ask Your Guides Oracle Cards, by Sonia Choquette

Ask and It Is Given Cards, by Esther and Jerry Hicks

Daily Guidance From Your Angels Oracle Cards,
by Doreen Virtue

The Nodes of the Moon

Your North Node is listed according to your birth date.

9 Mar. 1935 – 14 Sept. 1936	Capricorn
15 Sept. 1936 – 3 Mar. 1938	Sagittarius
4 Mar. 1938 – 12 Sept. 1939	Scorpio
13 Sept. 1939 – 24 May 1941	Libra
25 May 1941 – 21 Nov. 1942	Virgo
22 Nov. 1942 – 11 May 1944	Leo
12 May 1944 – 3 Dec. 1945	Cancer
4 Dec. 1945 – 2 Aug. 1947	Gemini
3 Aug. 1947 – 26 Jan. 1949	Taurus
27 Jan. 1949 – 26 July 1950	Aries
27 July 1950 – 28 Mar. 1952	Pisces
29 Mar. 1952 – 9 Oct. 1953	Aquarius
10 Oct. 1953 – 2 Apr. 1955	Capricorn
3 Apr. 1955 – 4 Oct. 1956	Sagittarius
5 Oct. 1956 – 16 June 1958	Scorpio
17 June 1958 – 15 Dec. 1959	Libra
16 Dec. 1959 – 10 June 1961	Virgo
11 June 1961 – 23 Dec. 1962	Leo

24 Dec. 1962 – 25 Aug. 1964	Cancer
26 Aug. 1964 – 19 Feb. 1966	Gemini
20 Feb. 1966 – 19 Aug. 1967	Taurus
20 Aug. 1967 – 19 Apr. 1969	Aries
20 Apr. 1969 – 2 Nov. 1970	Pisces
3 Nov. 1970 – 27 Apr. 1972	Aquarius
28 Apr. 1972 – 27 Oct. 1973	Capricorn
28 Oct. 1973 – 9 July 1975	Sagittarius
10 July 1975 – 7 Jan. 1977	Scorpio
8 Jan. 1977 – 5 July 1978	Libra
6 July 1978 – 5 Jan. 1980	Virgo
6 Jan. 1980 – 24 Sept. 1981	Leo
25 Sept. 1981 – 16 Mar. 1983	Cancer
17 Mar. 1983 – 11 Sept. 1984	Gemini
12 Sept. 1984 – 6 Apr. 1986	Taurus
7 Apr. 1986 – 2 Dec. 1987	Aries
3 Dec. 1987 – 22 May 1989	Pisces
23 May 1989 – 18 Nov. 1990	Aquarius
19 Nov. 1990 – 1 Aug. 1992	Capricorn
2 Aug. 1992 – 1 Feb. 1994	Sagittarius

2 Feb. 1994 – 31 July 1995	Scorpio
1 Aug. 1995 – 25 Jan. 1997	Libra
26 Jan. 1997 – 20 Oct. 1998	Virgo
21 Oct. 1998 – 9 Apr. 2000	Leo
10 Apr. 2000 – 13 Oct. 2001	Cancer
14 Oct. 2001 – 14 Apr. 2003	Gemini
15 Apr. 2003 – 26 Dec. 2004	Taurus
27 Dec. 2004 – 22 June 2006	Aries
23 June 2006 – 18 Dec. 2007	Pisces
19 Dec. 2007 – 21 Aug. 2009	Aquarius
22 Aug. 2009 – 3 Mar. 2011	Capricorn
4 Mar. 2011 – 29 Aug. 2012	Sagittarius
30 Aug. 2012 – 18 Feb. 2014	Scorpio
19 Feb. 2014 – 11 Nov. 2015	Libra
12 Nov. 2015 – 9 May 2017	Virgo
10 May 2017 – 6 Nov. 2018	Leo
7 Nov. 2018 – 4 May 2020	Cancer
5 May 2020 – 18 Jan. 2022	Gemini

Index

Notes

Notes

Notes

Notes

Notes

Notes

HAY HOUSE PUBLISHERS

We hope you enjoyed this Hay House book.
If you would like to receive a free catalogue featuring additional
Hay House books and products, or if you would like information
about the Hay Foundation, please contact:

Hay House UK Ltd

292B Kensal Rd • London W10 5BE
Tel: (44) 20 8962 1230; Fax: (44) 20 8962 1239
www.hayhouse.co.uk

***

Published and distributed in the United States of America by:
Hay House, Inc. • PO Box 5100 • Carlsbad, CA 92018-5100
Tel: (1) 760 431 7695 or (800) 654 5126;
Fax: (1) 760 431 6948 or (800) 650 5115
www.hayhouse.com

Published and distributed in Australia by:
Hay House Australia Ltd • 18/36 Ralph St • Alexandria NSW 2015
Tel: (61) 2 9669 4299; Fax: (61) 2 9669 4144
www.hayhouse.com.au

Published and distributed in the Republic of South Africa by:
Hay House SA (Pty) Ltd • PO Box 990 • Witkoppen 2068
Tel/Fax: (27) 11 706 6612 • orders@psdprom.co.za

Distributed in Canada by:
Raincoast • 9050 Shaughnessy St • Vancouver, BC V6P 6E5
Tel: (1) 604 323 7100; Fax: (1) 604 323 2600

***

Sign up via the Hay House UK website to receive the Hay House
online newsletter and stay informed about what's going on with
your favourite authors. You'll receive bimonthly announcements
about discounts and offers, special events, product highlights,
free excerpts, giveaways, and more!
www.hayhouse.co.uk